FIND YOUR WAY HOME

FIND
YOUR WAY
HOME

A New Play by
JOHN HOPKINS

NELSON DOUBLEDAY, Inc.
Garden City, New York

As produced on Broadway by Rick Hobard. It opened at the Brooks Atkinson Theatre, New York City, N.Y. on January 2nd, 1974 with the following cast:

Julian Weston	MICHAEL MORIARTY
David Powell	JOHN RAMSEY
Alan Harrison	LEE RICHARDSON
Jacqueline Harrison	JANE ALEXANDER

Directed by	EDWIN SHERIN
Setting by	WILLIAM RITMAN
Lighting by	MARC B. WEISS
Costumes by	THEONI V. ALDREDGE

ACT I

A SMALL FLAT in a large town in the south of England.

The main room of the flat is medium-sized, on the ground floor of the house, an old house, with high, decorated ceilings. Down right the long, angle-shaped window overlooks a run of large gardens, back to back, stretching a barrier against the traffic noise from the main coast road, which runs past the front of the house.

The room is furnished with the dreary and conventional cheap furniture common to furnished flats. It is only rescued from total depression by a variety of personal touches.

A footlocker sits down right. In the nook in front of the window stands a dining table with a straight chair at the end of it and another at the upstage end. An armoir with JULIAN's sweater and other clothes in it stands against the right wall. At a right angle to this and going upstage is the kitchen area. This consists of a small counter with two open shelves on the downstage side. The first shelf has magazines on it and the bottom shelf holds tan place mats. There is a sink next to this and an icebox with a counter on top next to the sink. On this counter is a dish drainer and an electric tea kettle. A dish cloth is draped over the

tap in the sink and a dish towel is on the downstage end of the counter. A wastebasket is on
the floor between the armoir and the counter.
There are two cabinets with three shelves each
on the kitchen wall. Dishes, cups and saucers,
glasses, silverware and coffee as well as other
kitchen things are in them. There is a dripolator
coffee pot near the tea kettle. Upstage center is
the door into the hall which leads to the front
door. On the wall opposite the kitchen is a mirror
and two coat hooks above it. At right angles to
this wall is the door to the bathroom. Next to
this door is a photo-montage of faces on the wall.
Some of the faces are famous actors and film stars,
singers. Some of the faces have been cut roughly
out of newspapers and a very few stare out of
glossy photographs, smiling and posed. The faces
are jumbled together without recognizable pattern. Some of the photographs are pinned to the
wall. Some of them are stuck there with Scotch
tape. A bed has been pushed against this wall,
using the wall as a substitute bed-head. Two pil-
lows with grey covers, two grey sheets, and a
brown blanket lie under a blue print bedspread.
At the foot of the bed is a blanket chest with
two clean blue pillow covers and two clean blue
sheets. JULIAN's white socks are also there. At
right angles to the montage wall is a mirror. At
right angles to this is another wall with a table
in front of it. On this table sits a small alarm
clock and a lamp. In the middle of the stage left
wall is a fireplace with a gas heater in it. On the
mantel sit two speakers for the stereo. Over the

mantel hangs a mirror. Upstage of the fireplace
are shelves filled with a wide range of books. Some
of them are hardback; art books, illustrated books
about the great houses of England, books on the
history of costume design. There are also shelves
filled with paperback books, which look almost
brand-new. One shelf holds a stereo unit with
records on the upstage side of it. There are also
some records on the floor in front of the shelves.
Downstage of the fireplace is a small table with a
lamp and ashtray on it. Downstage of this table is
an old straight-back armchair. Down center
there is a chair, contemporary in design, luxuri-
ous and obviously an addition to the furniture
the landlady has provided. It has a footstool in
front of it. A small round table with an ashtray
and matches is on the right side of the chair.
The room is lit mainly from these table lamps,
a lamp that hangs over the bed and a chandelier
that hangs from the ceiling center. Holiday posters with sun-bright vistas of golden sky and blue
sea are pinned to the walls of the room, inter-
spersed with pop art posters in psychedelic de-
signs. Everything is tidy and, within the compass
of the room, comfortable.

It is eight o'clock in the evening.

There is a rock LP playing on the record player.
On the upstage end of the dining table, a mat has
been placed with a dinner plate on it. There are
crumbs on the plate as well as a knife, fork, spoon
and rumpled paper napkin. There are crumbs on
the table as well.

JULIAN WESTON is lying on the floor in front of

the fire, his arms crossed on his chest, his body stretched straight and rigid.

WESTON is twenty-three years old, just below average height, slender, with very blond hair.

Slowly, WESTON raises his head and shoulders, tucking his chin down against his chest. When HE feels his stomach muscles pull tight, HE holds the position for a silent count of eight and then lowers his head and shoulders to the floor.

WESTON

Love! Darling, you don't know the meaning of the word.
(DAVID POWELL *is sitting in the leather chair.* POWELL *is thirty years old.* HE *has broad shoulders and a tough, slender physique.* HE *has thick-growing, brown hair cut relatively short.* HE *is wearing an open-necked shirt and brown corduroy pants*)
'Wham, bam and thank you, mam!'
(*The telephone starts to ring.* WESTON *lowers himself slowly to the floor and rolls on to his side looking up at* POWELL. POWELL *smiles amiably at* WESTON)
You're a lazy bastard.
(*The telephone is on the floor downstage end of the bed.* WESTON *picks up the receiver*)
Hello.
(*Silence.* WESTON *picks up the telephone and carries it to left of the center chair.* HE *puts the receiver against* POWELL'S *ear*)

POWELL

Can't hear . . .
(POWELL *seems to produce words from a distance, reluctantly, with a visible effort*)

WESTON

Listen. Listen carefully . . .
>   (*Silence*)

POWELL

Still can't . . .

WESTON

Breathing?

POWELL

>   (*Harshly*)
Nothing.

WESTON

Probably frightened him off. Silly bitch!
>   (*Puts the receiver against his ear and lis-
>   tens*)
Oh, well. 'Bye, love.
>   (*Silence.* WESTON *shakes his head, crosses
>   to chest, puts phone on floor, sits on chest
>   and then looks coldly along the length of
>   POWELL's legs, up at his face*)

POWELL

>   (*Quietly*)
You can look, baby—but you mustn't touch.
>   (*Silence*)

WESTON

Cheap and nasty, aren't you?

POWELL

You want to change the record?

WESTON

I didn't say you should move in, you know. I had a sort
of more temporary arrangement in mind.

POWELL

(*Quietly*)

You ask people in—you want they should take care of you, when it's dark and you're afraid—you can't just—you know?—when it's got light again and you're not frightened any more—tell them 'out'. You going to change the record?

(*Silence*)

WESTON

When I went off to work this morning I sort of thought—you might—well, have something to do—somewhere to go?

POWELL

No.

WESTON

You don't work?

POWELL

I don't work.

WESTON

How d'you keep—the wolf from the door?

POWELL

I don't—if I can help it. This is comfortable. Really—the most . . . comfortable—chair I think I've ever sat in—had the pleasure . . .

(*Silence*)

Hmm.

WESTON

Yes, it is.

POWELL

How d'you afford—something . . .

(*Silence*)
Present?

Yes.

(*Rises, crosses to stereo, moves needle to
another band, turns volume control up,
turns into the room*)

POWELL

Someone—loves you a lot—giving you presents—fancy
presents like this.

(*The sound is loud*)

Hey, Julie—no. Let's have something gentle—you know
—peaceful.

WESTON

(*Harshly, crosses downstage*)

You don't like this—get up—get off your fat backside—
find something you do like. For God's sake, David—you
make me sick.

(POWELL *sits forward and swings his legs
off the foot stool, onto the floor.
Half-laughing*)

David?

(POWELL *rises.* WESTON *backs away as*
POWELL *walks forward*)

I didn't mean—hey!—you know me—you know—er—
nothing personal—right?

(POWELL *stands watching* WESTON *following his movement around the room staring
at him*)

Well—like you said—things to do!

(HE *crosses down to center table, picks up
ashtray, crosses to trash can, empties tray,
returns it to table*)

Lots of things—must keep busy—yes? Busy hands make light work—or something—the devil finds hands for idle work—hands, knees and up your daisy!

(POWELL *walks to the record player and bends forward, takes needle off record, cutting off the sound in mid-phrase.* HE *rests his hands on the downstage shelf, letting his head roll forward onto his chest*)

Here.

(*Crosses downstage of* POWELL)

Let me.

(*Takes the stub of the cigarette carefully from* POWELL'S *fingers*)

What you do with your mind—that's your business.

(*Pressing the stub flat in the ashtray on the downstage left table*)

My furniture—that's something else.

(POWELL *reaches out suddenly and catches hold of* WESTON'S *arm.* HE *holds it tightly, backs* WESTON *to below chest, the fingers pressing into the flesh and marking it white.*

WESTON *watches* POWELL *calmly, without showing visible reaction to the pain*)

Well? If you don't want the goods—you know?—don't muck 'em about.

POWELL

You bother me, Julie. All the time—fussing—you bother me.

WESTON

You bore the shit out of me.

(*Silence*)

POWELL

You want to fuck?

WESTON

Not particularly.
(Silence)
And now—if you don't mind—

POWELL

It's colder. Isn't it getting colder?

WESTON

(Harshly)
Will you let go!
(POWELL *lets go of* WESTON's *wrist.*
WESTON *crosses above center chair to din-*
ing table)

POWELL

(Quietly)
Times—and you like to be hurt.

WESTON

Ha!

POWELL

I was reading about that—people—hurting you.

WESTON

Reading? Reading what? What d'you mean?

POWELL

Int'resting. All that stuff. Better than books.
(Silence. WESTON *opens the door of the*
armoir and crouches in front of it. HE
reaches into the armoir and pulls out a
folder. HE *looks at the mass of notebooks*
stacked inside it)

WESTON

You bitch. You rotten, filthy bitch. You cunt!

POWELL

(*Crosses to center chair, knee on upstage
arm*)
You don't have secrets—I mean—there isn't anything
you have to hide. It's like—I've been inside your head.
Inside your body—now—inside your head.

WESTON

(*Shuts armoir door*)
You must've known—surely!—reading—couldn't you see?
I didn't mean anyone should read . . .

POWELL

I wanted you last night. Tonight!—The way I feel tonight—what I know about you—what happens—thinking
. . . If you didn't mean anyone should read it—how
come you wrote it all down. Couldn't you just as well remember—keep it in your head?
(WESTON *crosses, sits on foot locker, holding folder close*)

WESTON

I didn't mean anyone should read it.

POWELL

(*Crossing below armoir*)
Someone—you wanted someone to read it. Maybe not
me . . .

WESTON

Not you.

POWELL

No—maybe not, but someone—yes?

Julie?
    (*Silence*)

    (HE *crosses and kneels beside* WESTON *and puts an arm across his shoulders, pulling him close towards him, holding him tight*)
I'm sorry, Julie.
    (HE *rubs a hand down* WESTON's *arm, comfortingly*)
You have to understand—reading those books—it seemed like a chance to know you—get to know you—and I couldn't stop myself . . . I've watched you—days and weeks. You must've seen me—you must've known. Didn't you know? Days—and I've wanted just to come and knock on your door—nights—the nights weren't any easier. And then—last night . . .

WESTON

    (*Cold, pulls away, crosses to below armoir*)
Last night, darling—I needed something warm in bed with me—something beside me—something I could touch —reach out and touch—if I woke in the night and I was scared—something—there—in the darkness—anything, darling—man, woman or dog.
    (*Crosses to bed, puts folder under mattress. Then rises, facing* POWELL)
You think I'm going to let you fuck me? I mean—now! What are you? Some sort of raving maniac! I wouldn't let you fuck me—as long as you live—one thing you have to know—you'll never—ever, ever, ever—get into me again.

POWELL

    (*Rises, crosses below armoir*)
Don't fight me, Julie. Not tonight. Couldn't it be gentle? I mean—last night—we did that whole thing . . .

WESTON

(*Right of chest*)

Do you want to know about last night? You talk like it
was something special. Darling—I've had more satisfaction eating an over-ripe banana—sucking on a stale blood
orange. Truthfully, I've had fellas make you look like a
girl.

(POWELL *crosses to above center chair,
reaching for* WESTON *who crosses below
center chair to right of it.* POWELL *turns
toward him*)

You don't coordinate too well. Must be all those nights—
thinking about me—having yourself—sitting in your dark
and dirty little room—chasing me around your dark and
dirtier little mind.

POWELL

(*Lunges at* WESTON, *between center chair
and footstool, loses his balance and falls
across small table center knocking it over.
HE rolls onto the floor downstage right*)

Come here.

WESTON

(*Below armoir*)

Go fuck yourself!

(*Silence.*

POWELL *rolls onto his back*)

Silly bitch!

(*Above center chair*)

Go away—will you? Please! You want to get into me—
you'll have to do better than that.

POWELL

I've been into you already—remember?

WESTON

(*Picks up table and replaces it, picks up ashtrays and matches and puts them on table*)

Doesn't establish property rights. Is that what you thought? Darling—if I can't do any better—if the best I can expect—the rest of my life . . .

(*The doorbell rings*)

I'll shoot myself in the head. Will you please get up and get the hell out of here?

(*The doorbell rings again.*

WESTON *crosses up center*)

I'm not—if you'll pardon the expression—playing hard to get—just—I want you to get out—go home—have yourself —you're not having me.

(*Walks to the door, opens it, exits. Silence.*

POWELL *stands up, pulling at his trousers and generally making himself more tidy.*

HE *crosses down left center.*

WESTON *appears in doorway, looks in. Turns back to hall, enters and stands right of the door.*

Quietly*)

Come in.

(WESTON *steps back from the door and watches* ALAN HARRISON *walk into the flat.*

HARRISON *is forty-seven years old.* HE *smiles easily, a smile which protects the eyes from showing too much pain, the face from seeming too vulnerable.*

POWELL *watches* HARRISON *as* HE *walks into the room.*

HARRISON *sees* POWELL *and stops.* HE

glances around at WESTON *quickly and then looks back at* POWELL)

HARRISON

I'm sorry. I didn't mean to disturb you—er—interrupt anything.

WESTON

(*Casually*)
You know my brother, don't you?

HARRISON

No, I don't think . . .

WESTON

(*Crossing, closing door, crossing right of bed*)
Surely?

POWELL

No. We've never met. I'd certainly remember.

WESTON

Well—Davy . . . this is Alan Harrison—a friend of mine —an old friend. I haven't seen him . . .
(*Silence*)
How long is it?

HARRISON

I don't think it's so very long. Six months—maybe—a little longer.

WESTON

Longer. Almost a year.

HARRISON

Is it? Well—if you say it is—I imagine . . .

WESTON

Almost a year.
> (HARRISON *looks at* POWELL, *glances at center chair, crossing to dining table*)

HARRISON

You've changed things around—haven't you?—moved the furniture . . .

WESTON

Yes.

HARRISON

I thought so. I wasn't sure . . .

WESTON

A year is really quite a long time—can be—a long time.

POWELL

> (*Smiling*)

Julian's really quite the little homemaker, isn't he? I don't know how he can afford all these expensive things.

WESTON

> (*To* HARRISON)

Are you staying? How long are you staying?

HARRISON

I don't know.

POWELL

Would you like something to drink?

WESTON

There isn't anything to drink.

POWELL

I can go out.

HARRISON

No—thank you—really. It doesn't matter.

WESTON

Take off your coat. Sit down.

POWELL

Yes. Make yourself comfortable. How is it out there? Still raining?

HARRISON

No. It's quite pleasant. A little heavy—I think perhaps it might . . .

WESTON

You should get home, Davy—before it starts.

POWELL

I don't mind the rain. It's good for the complexion. Isn't that what they say?

HARRISON

You don't live here?

POWELL

Oh, no. I'm just visiting. Keeping an eye on my baby brother. Seeing he doesn't get into trouble.
 (*The telephone rings*)
I'll get it.
  (HE *sits down on chest and picks up the*
  receiver. HE *listens for a moment, and then*
  looks up at WESTON)
I think it's for you.
  (HE *holds the receiver out to* WESTON.
  WESTON *takes the receiver and puts it to*
  his ear.
  HARRISON *watches the* TWO MEN *standing*

*together, sensing the understanding be-
tween them, controlled and invisible, but
clearly present in their attitudes*)

WESTON

You must have the wrong number. There's no one living
here called—what did you say?—Wilkinson!
(HE *looks at* POWELL)
Sorry.
(*Puts the receiver back on the telephone.*
POWELL *puts his hand on* WESTON's *hand.*
WESTON *sits on his heels*)

POWELL

(*To* WESTON)
I thought he said Weston.
(*To* HARRISON)
I could've sworn.

WESTON

He didn't.

POWELL

Easy enough mistake to make. It was such a bad line—I
could hardly hear him.
(*To* HARRISON)
Very breathy voice.

WESTON

Davy—why don't you tell Dad I'll look in this weekend—
some time this weekend.

POWELL

That's a promise?

WESTON

Yes—a promise.

POWELL

I'll tell him.
(HE *releases* WESTON's *hand*)

WESTON

(*Rising, cross above center chair*)
Not the whole weekend.

POWELL

He'll be so pleased.

WESTON

Tell him that—so he won't be disappointed.

POWELL

You know how much he looks forward to you coming.

WESTON

He shouldn't expect more than he can have from me.

POWELL

It's the only pleasure he has left.

WESTON

For God's sake, Alan—will you sit down? If you're staying—I mean—are you staying?
(HARRISON *shakes his head in doubt*)

POWELL

All this family gossip. I'm afraid it's very boring.

HARRISON

I thought your father was dead?

POWELL

No. What made you think—Dad! He wouldn't like to
know—Julian—did you say . . .

HARRISON

I thought you told me.

WESTON

Mum—I told you—Mum's dead. A couple of years ago that was. Dad's all right.

POWELL

Never better.
(*Rises*)
Goodbye, Mr. Harrison. I wish I could stay longer, but I can see Julian wants you all to himself. Got things to talk about. A year—did you say it was a year?
(*Crossing to* WESTON)
A lot can happen in a year. A person can change in a year—almost completely. I mean—sometimes—you might hardly recognize them—
(*Hand on* WESTON's *shoulder*)
Meeting them again.
(WESTON *takes* POWELL's *hand off shoulder.* POWELL *hangs on*)

WESTON

I'll see Davy to the door—yes? I won't be a minute.

HARRISON

Plenty of time.

POWELL

(*Abruptly*)
That's a promise—about the weekend?

WESTON

A promise.

POWELL

(*Smiling*)

One thing about Julian—never breaks a promise. Always know—if he makes a promise, he's going to keep it.

WESTON

Yes.

HARRISON

Goodbye.

POWELL

(*To* HARRISON)
Enjoy yourself.
(*To* WESTON)
We'll be thinking about you—
(*To* HARRISON)
Dad and me.
(WESTON *opens the door and the* TWO MEN
walk out of the flat.
Silence.
WESTON *walks into the flat.* HE *stands in
the doorway for a moment, and then shuts
the door behind him*)

WESTON

(*Up center*)
I thought you said—when I saw you last—didn't you say
—I'd never see you again?

HARRISON

No. I said—I would never see you again.
(*Silence. Smiling*)
There is a difference.

WESTON

(*Harshly*)
Either way—what are you doing here now? What do you
want?

HARRISON

I want to see you.

WESTON

(*Crossing above center chair*)
You didn't think—would I want to see you? You didn't
ask yourself . . .

HARRISON

Yes.

WESTON

You could have phoned.

HARRISON

I thought—if I phoned . . .

WESTON

I might say—no? I might—just possibly—tell you—go to
hell?

HARRISON

Yes.

WESTON

Right. Damn' right!
(*Silence. Quietly*)
Go to hell.

HARRISON

Yes.

WESTON

You're so understanding. You always were. Sort of a
bloody sponge! Let them say—anything—it's only right—
everybody's right—mea culpa—yes? Bastard!
(*Silence*)
Can't you sit down? I mean—if you're going to stay?
How long can you stay?

HARRISON

That's up to you.

WESTON

(*Violently*)

Oh, for God's sake! How can you say—look—if it's up to me—now—bloody go now—and don't come back. Don't come crawling in here with all this humble shit! You went away. You said—end—dead end. Goodbye—once more, good night—you said that. You said—remember?— it isn't possible.

(*Quietly*)

Didn't you say that?

(*Abruptly*)

Didn't you?

HARRISON

Yes, I did.

WESTON

Will you sit down?

(HARRISON *walks deliberately across downstage to a dingy, brown leather chair downstage of the fireplace.*)

(*Laughing*)

Oh, God—dear God! You're too much. Altogether—you know?—too bloody much. Do you know what that does—

(*Crosses to chest*)

D'you have any idea? 'I mustn't take anything for granted'—right?

(*Sits on chest*)

'I mustn't sit in my own chair. He might think . . .' You're so noble. Has anyone told you? Understanding— like I said before—reticent and sensitive—like five ele- phants in ten pairs of hob-nail boots. Sit in your own chair, will you?

(*Silence.* HARRISON *walks across to door, hangs coat and hat on hook, crosses to the chair and sits down on it*)
You look tired.

HARRISON

(*Smiling*)
Older?

WESTON

Yes—older, I suppose. Tired. Working too hard?

HARRISON

No.
(*Silence*)
Why did you leave the firm?

WESTON

What did you expect me to do?

HARRISON

I don't want to feel you had to leave—because—you and I—because . . .

WESTON

Oh, my love—your battered, beautiful, bleeding heart! I would have left long before, if it hadn't been for you. Most of the time I hated the place and everybody working there. What was I? Sort of a glorified office boy— right? Do this—do that—fetch the tea, lad—shit!—and get anything wrong—like I'd raped the Mother Superior. Didn't I ever tell you? Anyway, I've got a much better job now.

HARRISON

What's that?
(*Silence*)

WESTON

I don't want to talk about it.

HARRISON

Why not? Where are you working? What're you doing?

WESTON

Most of the time, love—I mean—my main preoccupation
—waiting for Mr. Right to come along—riding his great,
white charger, wearing his silver, shining armour and
waving his ten foot lance eagerly in my direction. What
I do is my affair entirely and nothing to do with you.

HARRISON

No.

WESTON

What are you doing here?

HARRISON

I came to see you.

WESTON

You want to go to bed?
        (*Silence*)
You always did. Hardly inside the door and it was—
'Take off your clothes—get into bed'—and getting out
again—'Sorry, love—can't stay long tonight—they're expecting me home early.'
        (*Silence.*
        HARRISON *takes out cigarette and lighter*)
How are they all at home? I should have asked. How
very forgetful of me! What's-her-name—your loving, for-
giving wife—how is she?

HARRISON

        (*Lights cigarette*)
Jackie . . .

WESTON

(*Harshly*)
I know what her name is.
(*Silence*)

HARRISON

She's well.

WESTON

And the children—how are they?

HARRISON

They're all right.

WESTON

Were they happy—getting you back? No, of course not. They didn't ever know you'd left—right? 'Course you didn't leave—physically—leave!—did you? That's the important thing. Presence—physical presence—never mind where the head is—where the thoughts go—the body— walking into the house at night—playing with the kids— sitting at dinner—in front of the telly—lying in bed— maybe—fucking—yes?

HARRISON

I wanted to leave them. I thought I could. I wasn't as strong—I wasn't—strong enough.

WESTON

You left me.

HARRISON

I thought I was.

WESTON

I think—it took strength—didn't it? Leaving me?

HARRISON

It was so easy.

WESTON

Bastard!

HARRISON

Isn't it always easy—running away?

WESTON

Oh, yes—I remember. Christ Almighty—yes! You're going to explain to me, aren't you—why it was easy—leaving me—difficult—going back to them—and why you had to do the difficult thing—right? You bloody martyr-saint!
(*Rises, crosses center*)
I have to understand—accept—it was easy to leave me—you—are going to make me understand. You—go fuck yourself!
(*Crossing, sits on bed.*)
(*Silence*)
You always make me feel stupid—in bed and I make you feel good—then—you can be generous. You can show me —love. You can give—and not explain—make me understand all the giving means—to you—to me—the meaning! I don't give a shit!
(*Silence*)
I have changed. Things—have changed. I'm not sure there's any place for you here. I don't think it exists any more. I think it was smashed—I think—we questioned too much—smothered—whatever it was—love—and now—there's nothing left. Truthfully, I think you should just go away.
(*Silence.* HARRISON *puts cigarette out, rises, crosses right of center chair to up center*)

HARRISON

Can I tell you something—first—before I go? I will go—if you want me to—if you send me away.

WESTON

That isn't fair.

HARRISON

I came to say something I didn't say that night—something I couldn't say. It was bad enough already.

WESTON

Yes.

HARRISON

I didn't want to make it worse by telling you I needed time to think. I needed time—to find out if I had to stay with them—if I could stay with them—and if I couldn't—then—what else to do.

WESTON

You didn't say anything about thinking.

HARRISON

No.

WESTON

You went away. You didn't tell me you might come back —when you'd had time to think.

HARRISON

I didn't know.

WESTON

I would have waited.

HARRISON

I couldn't ask you to wait . . .

WESTON

I wish you had.

HARRISON

(*Crosses toward* WESTON)
. . . until I knew—until I was certain . . .

WESTON

(*Quietly*)
Oh, God.

HARRISON

. . . I couldn't.
        (*Silence*)

WESTON

You should've—really, love—that's what you should have
done.
        (*Rises, crosses to kitchen, glass and
        Scotch bottle from cabinet*)
I need a drink.

HARRISON

(*Counter-crosses left*)
There's something else I want to say.

WESTON

Couldn't it wait? I'm having a certain amount of trouble
accepting the story so far—much more excitement—I
might just faint away. You know how susceptible I am
to stories of mystery and suspense.
        (*Drops Scotch bottle into trash can*)

HARRISON

Now—I am certain.
        (*Silence*)
I wanted to tell you.

WESTON

(Crossing, leans against side of armoir)
You're certain?

HARRISON

Yes.

WESTON

(Brightly)
Well—that only leaves me to ask . . .
(Shakes his head)
I don't want to know.
(Silence)
Certain about what?

HARRISON

(Crossing toward WESTON*)*
I want to live with you. Live here—with you—live any-where.

WESTON

No. You can't—Christ! Oh, Christ!

HARRISON

(Crossing and reaching out for WESTON*)*
Julie!
*(*WESTON *pulls away from* HARRISON*, stumbling backwards)*

WESTON

Get away from me.
*(*HE *crosses below armoir to upstage of up-stage chair in nook. Angrily)*
Do you know what you're saying? God in heaven—it isn't—happening. I don't believe . . .
(Silence)
Live with me?

HARRISON

Yes.

WESTON

Damn you!
(HE *brings his hands up to his mouth and
starts to cry*)

HARRISON

(*Helplessly, crossing below armoir*)
Please—Julie—I didn't mean . . .
(HE *walks hesitantly towards* WESTON)

WESTON

(*Crossing below to stereo*)
Don't come near me. Don't—most of all!—don't touch
me.
(*Silence*)

HARRISON

Shall I go away?

WESTON

I don't want you to go away.

HARRISON

I can come back. We can talk tomorrow. I don't want to
upset you.

WESTON

Did you think—I suppose . . . Yes, you did. You thought
I'd be just enchanted. Fall into your arms with shrill
squeals of delight. Isn't everyone simply ravished when
you walk into their dreary lives?

HARRISON

(*Smiling*)

I thought you'd be happy, rather than sad.

WESTON

Time passes, Alan.

(*Crosses below to dining table*)

People have to live the best way they can.

(*Picks up plate, napkin, silver, glass, mat,
and crosses to kitchen. Puts mat on bottom
counter of shelf, glass on counter, silver in
sink, wash plate, put in drainer*)

I don't think it's very practical, love. No—I don't think
it's a good idea—you—moving in here. For one thing—my
landlady would never approve. She gives me a pretty
hard time as it is. And you—anyway—I hardly seem to
know you. Just the other day, I was trying to remember
what you looked like. I got you confused with a whole
bunch of other people.

(*Brightly, crosses left of armoir*)

Sorry about that—still—it's better you know the worst—
rather than go on—hoping. The best thing—truthfully—
very much the best thing—we should say—goodbye—
and forget this whole thing happened.

HARRISON

(*Coldly*)

How do you plan to forget it? You haven't done too
well so far—forgetting.

(*Crosses below* WESTON *to left of him*)

It's almost a year. You keep saying it is and I'm sure
you're right. It's as clear now as it was then—

(*Grabs* WESTON'S *wrists*)

clear and painful—isn't it?

WESTON

(*Controlled*)

Let go of me.

HARRISON

Why won't you even let yourself consider the possibility
of my living here—living with you?

WESTON

You're hurting my wrists.

HARRISON

Is there someone else? Was he really your brother? Your
father is dead. I'm sure he is. You told me he was.
      (*Silence*)
Is he your brother?

WESTON

      (*Pushing* HARRISON *left*)
Brother—sister—distant cousin from Australia—what the
hell difference does it make. I said he's my brother. As
far as you're concerned—he is.
      (*Breaks away, crosses to table. Silence*)
You have changed. You hurt me. You were angry—
maybe—jealous?—and you hurt me.

HARRISON

Why can't we talk?
      (WESTON *puts his hands to his face*)
Julie?

WESTON

      (*Seriously, crossing downstage*)
I can't trust you, love. You went away. You said you
wouldn't—all the same—you did.

HARRISON

      (*Crossing right of center chair*)
I tried to explain.

WESTON

I know—and you were very fair. You could've written a letter—phoned.

(HE *crosses to kitchen*)

You came and told me. 'Course, you would. That's part of the thing—

(*Switches kettle on, puts coffee from cabinet into dripolator*)

your whole thing—

(HARRISON *crosses, sits in center chair*)

a man stands straight—takes his medicine—faces up . . . I didn't understand. I hurt a lot—and I cried—after you left. I used to cry all the time.

(*Laughing*)

It got ridiculous. Buses and trains—restaurants—

(HE *crosses with dish cloth to table, sits in upstage chair, wipes crumbs off table*)

once—I was home—talking to my mother—I started to cry. I said I'd lost my job. I was worried about the rent. She gave me a couple of quid—patted me on the head and told me—'Don't worry.' Poor old thing. I wanted to tell her—'Alan's left me. Gone back to his wife.' Oh, God! Everything there was—I gave it to you—and you went away—and I didn't have it any more. I couldn't give it to anyone else—d'you understand? I gave it to you—that—whatever it is—inside thing—truthful—me thing—you don't even know you have. Left on your own—trying with someone else—you find—it doesn't happen—nothing happens. He's all the way inside you—everything's the same—seems to be the same—the noises in your head—the anger—all the struggling—violence—only—you don't feel—there isn't—love.

(*Rises, crossing to sink*)

I used to cry all the time.

(*Shakes out dish cloth*)
Isn't that ridiculous?
  (*Mocking. Dish cloth down on counter.*
  Turns kettle off)
Oh, you! God help us!
  (*Pours water from kettle into dripolator*)
You're a push-over for any sob story. You watch the old
movies on the telly—yes? Leslie Howard—painting his
last great masterpiece—
  (*Acts this out up center*)
struggling against blindness, insanity—and the men tak-
ing away all the furniture.
  (*Grabs dish towel from counter, puts it*
  on his head, crosses left of center chair,
  kneels)
Merle Oberon beside him—her arms outstretched—
'Don't take the canvas. Leave him the canvas. At
least . . .'
  (*Chin in hand, leaning on chair arm*)
Or was it Ronald Colman? You stand up when they
play the National Anthem—right? Stand in line to wave
at the Queen—all those good things! You really believe
Mary Magdalene went straight after He died—
  (*Rises, crosses to sit on chest, dish cloth in*
  lap)
didn't go back on the game? All this—you know—it's just
—will I go to bed with you? I will. I want to. I like going
to bed with you. We can get into bed and make love.
When it's dark—you go home—and no regrets. Something good we can both remember—and no regrets.
  (*Smiling*)
Like the song says.
  (*Silence*)
I promise I won't expect—afterwards—you won't have to
stay.

(*Abruptly*)

Alan—for God's sake! How bloody noble do I have to be? You want me—yes?

HARRISON

(*Harshly*)

No.

(*Doorbell buzzes. Silence. Doorbell buzzes.* WESTON *rises, exits front door.* HARRISON *rises.* WESTON *enters, picks up dripolator from counter*)
(*Crossing to door*)

I think I'd better go, Julie.

WESTON

(*Crosses with dripolator to table*)

God knows what that was all about! Some crazy lady— thought she wanted this flat.

HARRISON

We can't talk. We don't even seem . . . I don't think we even like each other very much.

WESTON

(*Crossing to kitchen*)

Did you have anything to eat?

(*Silence—cream, sugar, cup, saucer, spoon to table*)

No—you didn't. Oh, well—that's your bad luck. Davy ate just about everything I had—including tomorrow's lunch.

HARRISON

(*Takes hat from hook*)

Is he your brother?

(*Silence*)

Sorry. I shouldn't ask.

WESTON

No. He's not my brother.

HARRISON

Is he important?

WESTON

He's so unimportant—he hardly exists.

HARRISON

He was here.

WESTON

(*Sits in downstage chair, pours coffee*)
He was here last night as well—for the first time. Tonight—for the last time. If you'd come around just that
bit sooner, love—he might not have been here at all.

HARRISON

I couldn't come back any sooner.

WESTON

No.
(*Smiling*)
Well . . .

HARRISON

And the weekend? Something—you promised—for the
weekend.

WESTON

So—I'll break a promise.
(*Smiling*)
I'm not that bloody special, love—I can't break a prom-
ise.

HARRISON

(*Hangs hat back on hook*)
Why did you lie?

WESTON

Why d'you think?

HARRISON

(*Crosses downstage*)
You didn't want me to know?

WESTON

Right! Abso-bloody-lutely-right! Give the man a prize.
Any prize from the bottom shelf—if you'll pardon the expression!

HARRISON

What difference does it make—knowing or not knowing
—why should you care?

WESTON

Pride. There is such a thing . . . I'd rather . . .
(*Crosses below to fireplace*)
Christ!

HARRISON

(*Crossing by dining table*)
What? What is it?

WESTON

I'm defending myself. Bringing out excuses—all the jus-
tifications . . .

HARRISON

There's no reason . . .

WESTON

(*Harshly*)
I know that!
(*Silence*)
How long is it you've been here—and already . . . How
do you do that? What is it—makes me feel so guilty? In-

stant guilt! You make me feel I've committed sins I've never even heard of. Everything—a sin—deliberately done to hurt you—bruise your sweet sensitive soul. God in heaven—are you so pure?

HARRISON

You don't have to defend yourself.

WESTON

Have you been faithful? Forget what's-her-name?
　　(*Crosses center*)
I don't count her.
　　(*Silence*)
Male or female? Most likely female. Some dolly at the office. New—since I was there—right? Looked at you twice and read the signs all wrong? Thought you wanted her—the silly bitch—and not the all-consuming nothingness between her legs.
　　(*Crosses above center chair*)
Did you tell what's-her-name? No—of course not! Why should you? It wasn't anything you meant to last. No reason you should hurt—I know you—if it isn't going to last—if there's no danger she'll find out—surely, it's better—what the eye can't see . . . What did you tell the dolly? Did you tell her—'This is to do with me, love—nothing to do with you?' Did you say—'If I was more honest—I'd stay home and have myself—but that's so nasty, furtive, guilty and sordid—and this sweet, ugly sickness—having myself in you . . .'

HARRISON

No, Julie—don't . . .

WESTON

'. . . this is the game—part of the game . . .'

HARRISON

(*Crosses above center chair*)

Please!

WESTON

'. . . I'll use you—and you—use me . . .'

HARRISON

Don't do this—to us.

WESTON

(*Anguish*)

Stop me. Make me stop. I love you.

(*Silence. Quietly*)

Alan—I love you. I've been angry for so long and I was never angry. Lonely—yes—and sometimes—lost—not angry—with this almost uncontrollable desire to hurt—to torture—even kill! The times I've killed you—wanted to destroy—and always in such hideous . . .

(*Silence.* HE *crosses downstage left chair, sits*)

Why did you go away?

HARRISON

(*Quietly*)

I ran away, Julie—mostly from myself.

(*Silence*)

If what you are disgusts you—the man you are—how can you live with any hope of being—knowing—happiness—or peace? No—you can only punish—prove to yourself—yes—I am disgusting. There is some satisfaction . . .

(*Silence*)

I thought it was meant. I thought—this is the man you are—the life you've made—and now—accept it. What did you expect? What right have you—has anyone!—expecting the life they want—perhaps—think they deserve?

(*Smiling*)

I caught myself thinking—if I'm so special—and I am!—
how is it no one sees? I lived ten years—and every day
lies, deceit—and endless little insincerities. I had affaires
—pathetic, cruel affaires. Women, at first—then girls—
because the women asked—expected—more than I could
give them—time and consideration—and the girls—they
didn't take it seriously. They had the time to pass—and
passing it with me—it wasn't painful—sometimes boring,
I suppose—but there were compensations. I always
bought them presents—and they didn't know I wasn't really there—I wasn't ever there. Any more—I think—than
Jackie knew. There was excitement—running from bed
to bed—a sense of power—able to have—no—not any
woman I might choose—but I was careful and I chose
without much risk they would refuse and so—could tell
myself—with anyone I chose.

(*Silence*)

Much more important—sleeping with strangers—I could
make an answer to the question—why—with my wife—
with Jackie—why don't I feel desire—why can't I make
myself enjoy—why?—and in all the other beds—thinking
of her—I could tell myself—if anyone's at fault, it surely
isn't me.

(*Silence*)

I played so many games with truth I lost all sense of
honesty. Business trips—late dinners—

(*Crosses above to left of center chair*)

entertaining guests in town—visiting executives—I had a
madness in my head. I never told the truth to anyone—

(*Silence*)

Once—I arranged an evening on my own—with all the
same elaborate mechanism—time to think—time—to step
back and look at this whole distorted pattern of reality. I

found—there was no one in my life I trusted. No one I could let come close—no one could even understand—no one who knew the simple basic fact—my life—everything —was part of this same lie—this slight—but central!—divergence from the truth. I had contrived an absolute aloneness for myself. Why did I go away?

> (*Crosses, sits on chest*)

You have to understand, love—at that time—truthfully, I thought—That was the life I wanted—and most of the time—enjoyed it—It was a sort of death—but locked inside—keeping my head down and my eyes closed—I was happy—and why not! What's so much better here?—out here!—and I'm not happy—more alone—and all the time —aware!

> (*Silence*)

I did come here tonight—thinking we could make love— and right away—before we talked—before—anything!— make love. That was the fantasy—blanking out thought— and all consideration—just—the memory of every night we spent here.

> (WESTON *rises, crosses to* HARRISON, *hand to* HARRISON'*s head, caressingly*)

WESTON

We could do that. Why don't we? There's no reason why we shouldn't. Couldn't we, Alan—make love?

HARRISON

How do I make you feel guilty? You always seem to me— so innocent.

> (*The telephone starts to ring.* HARRISON *rises, crosses and sits in center chair.* WESTON *sits on chest, picks up phone*)

WESTON

Hello.

(*Silence*)
I'm sorry, love. You must have the wrong number . . .
That's all right. Goodbye.
      (*Puts the receiver down*)
Bloody telephone! You remember days you get a right
number.

HARRISON

You get your share of wrong ones.

WESTON

Yes.

HARRISON

Was it Davy?
      (*Silence*)

WESTON

      (*Harshly*)
No, it wasn't Davy.
      (*Stands up, crosses up center*)
If it had been Davy—I would've said—get stuffed and
knotted—will you? Stop messing me about.
      (*Viciously*)
Go fuck yourself!
      (*Silence*)

HARRISON

I'm sorry.

WESTON

      (*Bitterly*)
You're allowed. The whole charade was pretty stupid. I
don't know why—suddenly—it was so important you
should think he was my brother—something—anything—
but not—well—what he was.

HARRISON

Thank you.

WESTON

(*Crosses to bed, sits*)

Oh, no—now—that's taking chivalry too far—thanking me . . .

HARRISON

If it meant that much . . .

WESTON

D'you know what this party needs? Booze! I know that's what I need.

HARRISON

I thought you said there isn't a drink in the house?

WESTON

The pubs are open. Love—would you go down to the local? Buy us a bottle of scotch.

HARRISON

(*Feet on footstool*)

Do I have to? I don't want to move. It's warm here and I'm comfortable.

WESTON

Lazy—that's what you are.

HARRISON

I suppose—I don't feel much like a drink myself . . .

WESTON

Selfish—and lazy!

HARRISON

If you insist . . .

> (*Rises, crosses up center, hat and coat
> from hook, crosses downstage putting coat
> on*)

Julie—you're glad—yes?
> (*Silence*)

WESTON

Yes.

HARRISON

Why don't I want to go?

WESTON

> (*Rises, helps* HARRISON *with coat*)

I'm sorry he was here.

HARRISON

I won't be long.

WESTON

Alan, I'm not innocent, you know.

HARRISON

It'll be all right.

WESTON

The night you left—after you left . . .
> (*Silence. Briskly*)

I'll tell you all about it some time—if you really want to
hear. Go and buy the scotch.

HARRISON

Tell me about it.

WESTON

> (*Taking keys from pocket, hands them to*
> HARRISON)

Here. You'll need a key.

HARRISON

Thanks.

> (HARRISON *pulls the door open, looks at*
> WESTON, *walks out of the flat pulling the*
> *door shut quietly behind him.*
> WESTON *looks around the flat.*
> *Silence*)

WESTON

> (*Muffled*)

After you left—

> (WESTON *crosses to door, light switch off.*
> *Strips sheets and blankets off bed. Reaches*
> *for switch—turns on lamp over bed. Sits*
> *bed*)

I walked for an hour—longer—I don't know exactly. I
went to your house. I stood on the street and watched.
The lights went out downstairs. I saw you go to bed—
and when you switched the light out in your bedroom—
then—I went away.

> (*Silence*)

I sat in a cafe. It was one o'clock. A man spoke to me—
asked—was I on my own—and I said—yes, I was. We sat
for a while and talked and he said—would I go with him?
We left the cafe and we walked together—talking—he
was talking—and he said—would I let him fuck me? I
loved you, Alan.

> (*Silence*)

We went into a park and—yes—I let him fuck me. It was
cold and the grass was very wet. He held me—with his
hands around my neck. He hurt me—pushing into me.
His nails tore the skin across my neck. He talked and told
me all the things he'd do—but he came quickly and there

wasn't time. He left me then. He went away. He didn't
speak to me.

> (*Silence.* WESTON *pushes himself forward
> across the bed and stands up.* HE *reaches
> to pick up the blankets.* HE *stands in the
> middle of the room, holding them in his
> arms, pressed against his chest*)

I couldn't go back home. I asked a friend—did he have a
room? Could I sleep there—maybe on the couch? Come
on—he said—of course there's room—No reason we
should make you sleep in there—he said—the fire's gone
out and it's so bloody cold. You come and sleep with
me. I couldn't let him fuck me—and he said—what do
you think this is, love? You sleep here—you pay the rent.
I took him in my mouth. He came—and went to sleep. I
stayed there—but I couldn't sleep—and in the morning—
soon as it was light—I went away.

> (*Pulls one blanket free and spreads it
> clumsily across the bed.* HE *kneels beside
> the divan, fumbling with the blanket, try-
> ing to push it straight*)

Why did you leave me? Why did you go away? It's your
fault—your fault! God in heaven—why did you let me? I
didn't want to do those things. I didn't want to let them
fuck me. They were strangers. I didn't know their names.
Why weren't you here to stop me, Alan? If you'd been
here . . .

> (*Pushes himself to his feet and turns away
> from the bed.* HE *stumbles across the room
> towards the record-player and starts rec-
> ord*)

They were all friends—good friends—I knew them—really quite well—and they said—'Julie—we're having a
party. You're the guest of honour'—and they laughed. I

went to the party with them, and of course there wasn't
any party. It was a game they were playing with me—and
I knew. Love—I knew it was a game. I always knew!
I knew what they had planned and that was my game—
played against them—knowing—and letting it happen
anyway. They had this plan to rape me. Two of them
holding—two of them watching—one of them—and I
laughed. What did they think—what was there left to
rape? They thought they were so wicked—pulling off my
clothes—dissolute—depraved! 'Shit, darling—I've been
fucked' I said 'in dirty lavatories—but men would just as
soon fuck sheep. I've been spread across tables in trans-
port cafes . . . fucked in the dark by frightened little
men . . . fucked in broad daylight—nearly torn in
half . . .'
> (*The sound blasts out of the twin speak-
> ers.*
> *The door of the flat opens and* HARRISON
> *walks into the room, carrying a paper bag
> with a scotch bottle in it.* HE *pushes the
> door shut behind him.* HE *walks to counter,
> puts bag down, crosses to stereo, lifts arm
> off record, crosses to* WESTON.
> *Silence*)

HARRISON

What is it, Julie? For God's sake—what happened?

WESTON

Love me, Alan—please—make love.
> (WESTON *crosses to* HARRISON.
> THEY *embrace*)

CURTAIN

ACT II

One hour later.
   The room is almost dark.
   The only lights on are the lamp over the bed,
the lamp on the U.L. table and the lamp on the
D.L. table.
   HARRISON is sitting in the chair, with his legs
stretched across the foot stool. HE is wearing a
shirt and trousers. The shirt is open at the neck.
   WESTON is sitting on the bed, in his bathrobe,
holding a pillow.
   Silence.

WESTON

Love—

HARRISON

Yes.

WESTON

Since I left home I've always lived in rooms—hideous
furnished rooms—like this.

HARRISON

   (*Crosses up center to mirror*)
What's wrong with this?

WESTON

I want to live in some place really nice—some place belongs to me—
    (*Smiling*)
belongs to us—yes?

HARRISON

Yes.

WESTON

I'd like to make a home for you.
    (*The doorbell rings*)
Oh, for pity's sake! Do I have to answer?

HARRISON

    (*Crosses to upstage window*)
Will they go away?

WESTON

I don't know.
    (*Silence. The doorbell rings again.*
    WESTON *rises, crosses toward up center
    door*)
I'll have to answer. Can't let them wake my landlady—at
this time of night!

HARRISON

Put something on your feet.

WESTON

    (*Mocking, crosses to bathroom door, ex-
    its*)
Yes, Dad.

HARRISON

    (*Crosses below armoir*)
If it's someone you know . . .

WESTON

(*Off*)

It better be someone I know. A stranger—I might just punch in the mouth.

(WESTON *enters*)

What sort of time is this for strangers!

HARRISON

(*Crosses center*)

If you want to ask them in . . .

WESTON

I don't.

(*The doorbell rings again.*

WESTON *crosses to up center door, turns on lights*)

Bloody persistent, aren't they? Really—you think I'd ask anyone . . .

(*Silence*)

Oh, love.

(WESTON *shakes his head and walks out of the flat.*

HARRISON *crosses to down left armchair, picks up tie from back, puts it on, crosses to stereo, turns it down.*

The sound of the front door being closed.

HARRISON *turns to look across the room at the door, as it is pushed open.* WESTON *enters, stands right end of armoir.* JACQUELINE HARRISON *walks into the flat, stands up center.*

JACKIE *and* HARRISON *stare at each other across the room*)

(*Closes door behind* JACKIE, *then crosses to sink*)

She absolutely insisted you were here, Alan.

HARRISON

Jackie. What are you doing?

JACKIE

I followed you.
(*Silence*)

WESTON

Mrs. Harrison—wouldn't you like to sit down? You must be so tired—standing out there half the night. I know how exhausting that can be.
(JACQUELINE HARRISON *is forty-two years old*)
Let me take your coat?

JACKIE

No.

WESTON

Suit yourself.

HARRISON

I don't understand, Jackie. Followed me?

JACKIE

Who is he? What is happening?
(*Violently crosses downstage*)
You don't understand!

WESTON

(*Blandly*)
My name's Julian Weston. You two know each other already, don't you?
(*Silence*)

JACKIE

(*To* JULIAN; *quietly*)
Julie.

WESTON

My friends call me Julie—yes. It's sort of sweet, don't
you think?

JACKIE

                    (*To* HARRISON)
Julie?

WESTON

No. I'm Julie. That's Alan.

JACKIE

                    (*Shouting*)
Julie!

WESTON

Please—do you mind—Don't make too much noise. My
landlady . . .

JACKIE

                    (*Crosses below chest*)
He is Julie? He wrote those letters?
                    (*Silence*)

WESTON

Letters?

JACKIE

                    (*Desperately*)
Did he write those letters?

HARRISON

Yes.

JACKIE

I read them.

WESTON

My letters? You read my letters?
> (HARRISON *walks towards* JACKIE *and* SHE
> *backs quickly away from him, stumbling
> against the foot stool.* SHE *falls heavily
> across it and rolls on to the floor.*
> HARRISON *crouches beside* JACKIE, *reaching
> to take hold of her*)

JACKIE

> (*Screaming*)
Get away from me. Get away!

WESTON

Why did you let her read my letters? Why didn't you
keep them safe?
> (*Silence*)

JACKIE

> (*Viciously, gathering herself together*)
I thought at least you had a woman here. I didn't re-
alise . . .

HARRISON

> (*Reaches for her again*)
Here—let me help you.

JACKIE

> (*Rises, crosses away right*)
Don't touch me. Filth! You are—filthy!

WESTON

> (*At center chair*)
I have a feeling, love—this could be sort of ugly.
> (*Brightly*)
Tell you what—why don't we—right away now—all of us

—pull ourselves together? Stop behaving like children.
Remember where we are—and—God is always watching!
—all those good things—and before we start this—stop!
Why don't we do that?

JACKIE

You've been—to bed together?

WESTON

Could we do that?

JACKIE

You've been—what do you call it—surely not!—making
love?

WESTON

No, we couldn't.

JACKIE

Is that what you've been doing?

WESTON
(*Crosses behind* HARRISON)
Darling—if you can't get it—don't knock it.

HARRISON
(*Crosses, gets coat from down left chair,
crosses to* JACKIE)
Jackie—why don't you let me take you home?

JACKIE
(*Harshly. Backs away to dining table*)
When I want to go home, I'll find my own way—thank
you very much.

HARRISON

I don't see the point—staying here to fight.

JACKIE

Will it upset him? Is he sensitive—easily bruised?

WESTON

(*Crosses down left center*)

Alan—you can't just walk out of here.

HARRISON

(*Upstage of* JACKIE)

Be reasonable, Julie . . .

WESTON

You can't do that.

HARRISON

Try to understand.

WESTON

No.

HARRISON

I'll just take Jackie home.

WESTON

You won't come back.

HARRISON

Don't be ridiculous.

WESTON

You won't.

HARRISON

I have to talk to her. I can't talk here—with both of you . . .

JACKIE

(*To* HARRISON)

Do I make you feel uncomfortable?

WESTON
(*Crosses left of foot stool*)
It would've been all right—yes?—if you'd found him
with a girl?

JACKIE
It would have been more normal. It's always been a girl
before.

WESTON
How do you know?

HARRISON
(*Harshly*)
No—come on—will you? Stop it!

WESTON
Act like a gentleman—nice and polite? I'm not a gentleman—I'm not a man at all. Ask her. She'll tell you.

JACKIE
You make me feel sick!
(HARRISON *turns upstage*)

WESTON
(*Crosses downstage*)
Why? What's so special 'bout the way you fuck? You get
it in the front. I get it in the back. Sometimes—a bit of
both—and so do you. What makes it normal—done to you
—makes it so shameful—when it's done to me?

HARRISON
(*Crosses below to left of foot stool*)
Julie—shut up!

WESTON
(*Crosses above center chair to right of it*)

You take him in your mouth—right? Something he expects—and if you won't—maybe he'll go find someone else who will. Why—when you do it—good—and when I do it—evil, sick—depraved? I didn't ask you to come here.
> (*Turns to* HARRISON, *crosses up left*)

I didn't ask you to come back. Why don't you—yes!—if you want to—go away!

JACKIE

Is he always this hysterical?

WESTON
> (*Above center chair*)

You let her read my letters.

HARRISON

I didn't.

WESTON

I wrote them to you.

HARRISON

I wouldn't let anyone read your letters.

JACKIE

I should hope not. From a girl—they're pretty sickening to read—but from a man—disgusting!

HARRISON

Jackie—please?
> (*Crosses to stereo, turns it off*)

WESTON
> (*Crosses right center*)

I make you sick? You make me vomit blood! I know the life he has with you. I know the things you do to him. You think he hasn't told me?

JACKIE

(*Quietly*)

One thing—obviously—you don't know. How much he
hates a scene.

WESTON

I know how much he hates you. Each time he comes
here—each time we make love—he tells me—what it's like
with you. How nothing happens—just—the fantasies he
makes inside his head.

HARRISON

You make me feel ashamed.

WESTON

(*Harshly*)

You're going back with her.

HARRISON

(*Crosses up center*)

Whatever I do—how can that justify—trying to destroy
—saying things—deliberately to hurt . . .

WESTON

(*Laughing. Crosses toward* HARRISON)

I couldn't put a mark on her—much less destroy. She'd
have to take me seriously—admit I might exist. She'd
have to hear the things I say.

JACKIE

I can hear quite clearly.

WESTON

(*Crosses above center chair*)

No—you're reacting to a new idea—Alan can fuck a fella.
You don't see me—certainly, don't hear—just all the clut-
ter in your head—screaming and shouting—"How can

he do this to me? How can he make me feel so dirty?
How can he put himself—inside . . ." Have you got that
far? Or is it still—"What sort of idiot does this make me
—loving him—going to bed with him—letting him fuck
me—and all the time he wanted—this!"
(*Silence. Gently*)
Is that more like it?

HARRISON
(*Crosses downstage to foot stool*)
Jackie—I'll take you home.

WESTON
I've been there, darling—every time he went from me to
you—back into your bed—I had to think—"He'll fuck her.
Yes—of course he will. He has to." I told myself—he
couldn't want to—very likely I was wrong.

HARRISON
(*Sits on foot stool*)
What good does it do—talking like this?

WESTON
Because I'm stupid—and not sensitive at all—I put my-
self through all the messy business of your—making love.
Is that what you still call it? After all this time!

HARRISON
Julie—you must stop.

WESTON
(*Crosses above* HARRISON)
I want to save you, Alan. Presumptuous of me—yes, I
know—
(*Kneels left of* HARRISON)
and if I can't—maybe—protect a little. When she gets

you out of here, she'll be so sympathetic. She'll say
—"Darling, you're sick—a little bit insane"—no—some
much kinder word. Unbalanced! Meaning the same
thing—out of your bloody mind! She'll take you to a doc-
tor and they'll try to cure you—'cause they don't want
to think—they can't let themselves believe—you love me
'cause you love me . . . and the making love—something
we do because it makes us happy.
    (*Rises, crosses above* HARRISON *to above
    center chair*)
Look at her, love—she thinks we have some sort of orgy
here—and do forbidden things! She thinks you want to
fuck me 'cause it'd be different—sick—perverted—some
new kind of thrill! She thinks it can be cured—with help
—and the love of a good woman!
    (*Sits center chair*)
You won't make anything clear—taking her away—talking to her—telling her where you both went wrong and
why it's better you should separate—she knows all that.
    (*Rises, crosses left of* HARRISON)
Christ Almighty, Alan—aren't you here? You're sepa-
rated. Maybe you haven't told each other—you've been
separate for years.
    (*Embraces* HARRISON)
She has to know—you are in love with me—not 'cause
I'm a fella—'cause you are in love.
    (*Silence*)

JACKIE

    (*Calmly*)
Alan—I think he's asking you a question.
    (*Silence*)

WESTON

Why do you want him back?

JACKIE

Has he ever left?

WESTON

Didn't you tell her?

JACKIE

Isn't it obvious? He hasn't told me anything.

WESTON

You came here and you didn't—
(*Rises, crosses up center*)
what are you doing here?—you didn't tell her?
(HARRISON *puts head in hands*)

JACKIE

I simply thought you were a girl—another girl—and this time—for many personal and private reasons I won't discuss with you—I couldn't let him—get away with it.

WESTON

You followed him?

JACKIE

One of your letters told me where you lived—another had your name—a note I found—your telephone number.

WESTON

You looked at everything?

JACKIE

Everything I could find.
(*Silence*)

WESTON

(*Crosses above center chair, hand on back of it*)

Is this the way you always carry on? Playing at amateur detective? Catching them—in flagrante delicto—yes? Taking him home again—his tail—between his legs?

JACKIE

(*Crosses below armoir*)
It isn't—fucking—what you do together. You want to think it is—you want to call it that—all right, it isn't.

WESTON

(*Quietly*)
No.

JACKIE

He—uses you. He . . .
(*Silence*)

WESTON

Buggers me? Yes. Unless you would perhaps prefer to use some more refined and technical expression? Sodomy? You want to use these words—you have to say them with a little less concern—more casual, darling—
(*Backs* JACKIE *to table*)
'cause they are the truth of what we do together and they say more clearly what it means—to put yourself inside another human being—taking him—yes—and using him—for your own satisfaction. Is that what he does to you?
(*Crosses up center*)
That's what he does to me. It gives him pleasure and it makes me glad. I want him—using me.

HARRISON

(*Desperately*)
I want this all to stop.

WESTON

(Crosses to center chair, sits)
How do you think it will then? Do you anticipate—an
act of God!—in His mercy—reaching down to take you
up—out of this "earthly travail"? You and Christ—Moses
—and Isaiah!

JACKIE

Did you think you could walk out tonight and—what?—
write me a letter! I'm not coming home again. Give my
love to the children.

WESTON

You ran away.

HARRISON

I wanted time.

JACKIE

Is that what you wanted? Coming here?

WESTON

(Crosses down left chair)
You took time—leaving me—then—you had your time to
think—and decided to come back.

JACKIE

(Crosses right of foot stool)
Time to think? Think about what? Leaving a family
you've had for twenty years? How long did you take—
thinking about that?

WESTON

A year—almost.

JACKIE

Thinking—about you? And all that time—he hasn't had

JACKIE

Bastard!

HARRISON

. . . defenceless . . .

JACKIE

(*Crosses to* HARRISON)
You couldn't imagine living on your own. You never
have—how could you face it then? Alone! In six months
you'd be mad—or dead.

HARRISON

I am alone.

JACKIE

(*Turns downstage*)
Alan—please! You'll have us all in tears.

WESTON

You bitch!

JACKIE

(*Looks at* WESTON. *Then*)
You never let yourself be on your own for more than
twenty minutes—any day in your whole life.

WESTON

Look—if you really want to take each other through
your dismal marriage—day by day—apportioning praise
and blame—I would much rather you went home.

JACKIE

Would you like to see the letters Alan wrote to me?
        (*Crosses above center chair to below
        chest*)
Just ordinary letters—written with ordinary love and

foolishness. Nothing like the passion, violence and near hysteria you write about in yours. Would you like to see the—loving kindness—there can be between two people —friends for more than twenty years—and how much more between a man and woman who have been through that same intoxication you can write about so well?

(*Silence. Crosses upstage of* WESTON)

Would you like to see how much affection Alan has for me?

(*Silence*)

At best you share him with me—at worst—because of me—you'll lose him. It isn't easy—breaking the habits of more than twenty years. You think he won't remember? You think he won't regret? Some things—

(*Left center area*)

he must regret. How well can you cook? I cook really well. You keep your home quite tidy. Do you like to walk? Can you entertain yourself—he spends so many nights at work. Obviously—some of those nights he'll spend with you. He won't need to go elsewhere, will he? There's such a plentiful supply at home. But—only some —he does work hard—and he won't be able to take life easy now. With two homes to support—the children at their most expensive age. Happily—there won't be any more.

(SHE *turns to face him. Viciously*)

Of course, he won't come back to me. Perhaps, I wouldn't have him.

(*Silence*)

He can't stay here with you. You're the excuse he needs to leave me—his "grand amour!" He'll make you accept the guilt he cannot even recognize—and when he does— you think he'll stay? Surely—much easier—go on to someone else. Leave all the guilt with you and run away again. At his age—forty-seven—forty-eight next month—can he change completely—make himself into another man—and start again? Living with some other woman—just the guilt would cripple him—with you—the shame—contempt—disgust on people's faces—you think he won't despair?

WESTON

Go away. Alan—take her away.

JACKIE

Excitement has always been his one great stimulant— the novelty—the first infatuation. How long can you excite him? He does get bored. Have you had long enough to find out how easily? Have you had time to talk? What can you talk about? Except to tell each other how much you are in love—how brave, courageous—noble—you both are. All for love—and the world . . . You think he never was in love with me? Is that what he told you? He loved me—not only when we married—years after that and he still loved me. After his affairs began—
    (*Crosses upstage of* WESTON)
he still made love to me—still wanted me. You think he wasn't violent? Is that what he told you? He used to beg me—"Jackie—take me in your mouth."

HARRISON

You think I'm still the man you married.

JACKIE

No. I watched him
    (*Crosses to center chair, handkerchief from purse*)
come to pieces some ten years ago. I make the best of what small fragments I have left.

WESTON

I'd like you to continue this conversation in the peace and privacy of your own home. I've had enough.

(*Rises, crosses to bathroom door*)

I'm tired. I'd like to go to bed. Shut the door quietly as you leave. I want you both to go away.

JACKIE

(*Quietly*)

I was unfaithful once. It wasn't too successful. He didn't even like me. He didn't like you either.

WESTON

Please—will you go away?

JACKIE

(*Crosses above center chair to right center*)

I think that's how we came to go to bed.

WESTON

Alan!

JACKIE

We had so much to talk about.

WESTON

There's no point hanging on. There's nothing left. Why don't you just go home?

JACKIE

We spent the evening quietly. We talked. He took me out to dinner. It was all so ordinary.

HARRISON

(*Sits at table*)

I want to stay here.

WESTON

(*Opens bathroom door*)
It was a nice idea, love. It didn't work.

JACKIE

When he took me home—funny—it seemed so natural—
going to bed with him. Was he so very clever—or was I
—so inexperienced? Of course, I wanted him to love me.

WESTON

Before I get to screaming at you, Alan—will you go
away?
(*Silence.* JACKIE *looks at* WESTON. WESTON
exits)

JACKIE

When I woke up later, he was asleep. I couldn't think
why there was a face I didn't recognise—I couldn't understand—lying on the pillow next to me. I thought I
must be dreaming. In my mind—when I was unfaithful
—thinking about it—then, it was so fierce—explosive—
uncontrolled—and this—it didn't even seem important.
How can you tell one from any other, if it's always just
the same?
(*Silence.* WESTON *enters, gets socks from
chest, sits chest, puts on socks*)
Why don't we go home?
(*Picks up purse*)

HARRISON

I want to stay here.

JACKIE

I don't think you should. I don't think it's very sensible.
I'm tired. Can't we go home?

HARRISON

Why did you follow me?

JACKIE

I want to help you.

HARRISON

You couldn't let me go.

JACKIE

Really—do you want me to?

HARRISON

Would you believe me—if I told you—yes, I do?

JACKIE

(*Calmly*)

If there was any reason why I should—yes—I'd believe you.

WESTON

(*Puts on shoes*)

I think you should at least give it some thought. He might not be so careless next time—leave you so many clues. Let him go again—you might not find him quite so easily.

JACKIE

He wanted me to find him.

WESTON

Come and fetch him home? Yes—I think perhaps you're right. Still—maybe—another time.

JACKIE

(*To* JULIAN)

He won't come back to you.

WESTON

Darling—I wouldn't have him if he did. I'm much too good for him.

(*Rises, crosses to armoir, gets sweater, puts it on.*

JACKIE *counter-crosses below foot stool*)

It's sort of cold. I think I'll take a sweater. If that's the life you settle for, old love—must be the life you deserve —right? Don't we always get what we deserve?

(*Silence. Crosses to up center door, keys from counter, hat from hook*)

I'm going out. I'd rather you weren't still here when I get back. Oh—and switch the lights out. Somehow I feel I'm making some sort of exit—which is ridiculous. I mean—this is where I live—it was a nice idea. Take him home and keep him safe. If you can't stop him—nobody else can.

(WESTON *walks out of the flat and pulls the door shut quietly.*

Silence)

JACKIE

Some time ago I knew you were having an affair. As a matter of fact, I wanted to ask you—I mean—if anyone could help—you were unhappy—and I thought—

(*Embarrassed*)

probably I could help—if you'd just talk about it.

HARRISON

Talk to you about it?

JACKIE

(*Abruptly*)

You were hardly keeping it a secret! Moping about the

house. Betty asked me what was wrong. You think I couldn't guess. I've been married to you . . .

HARRISON

(*Harshly*)
Yes, I know how long.
(*Silence. Crosses above to down left center*)
I didn't want to talk about it.

JACKIE

And then—last week—either it was starting up again—or there was someone else—something—and I had to stop it.

HARRISON

You went to my desk and searched through all my papers.

JACKIE

You think I liked doing that?

HARRISON

I don't know. You did it.

JACKIE

I didn't want to find the bloody letters!

HARRISON

. . . A little while ago . . . I would have said it was impossible.

JACKIE

Yes—impossible. Well—I was younger—and I had a lot more hope.
(*Silence*)
Why didn't you leave me? I could have brought the children up. Why did we have the children? Fifteen

years ago! You must have known you meant to be unfaithful long before.

HARRISON

I never meant to be unfaithful.
  (*Silence*)

JACKIE

Would he mind—d'you think I could have a drink?

HARRISON

I didn't set out—
  (HARRISON *crosses to kitchen, two glasses
  from cabinet, scotches from the bottle on
  the counter.*
  JACKIE *puts purse on center chair, crosses
  to fireplace, takes coat off and puts it in
  down left chair*)
for God's sake!—what d'you think?—one day I made up
my mind—I'm going to be unfaithful. I didn't think—in
a million years—I couldn't imagine . . .

JACKIE

It isn't difficult, is it? I've always understood it's some-
thing anyone can do. Anyone gets married in the first
place. It doesn't count, does it—if you aren't married?
That isn't being unfaithful, is it? What is that called?
  (*Silence.* HARRISON *crosses to* JACKIE)
If it was so difficult for you—
  (*Smiling*)
I can believe it was!—you must have thought a lot about
it. Knowing you . . .
  (HARRISON *turns downstage.*
  Mocking.)
I'm not supposed to say that. Sorry. Let's say I've never

met you. I'll make no assumptions. I'll simply tell you
how you seem to me—tonight—as if I met you—tonight.
        (JACKIE *drinks some of her scotch*)
One thing—you don't seem queer.
        (*Silence*)
Why did we have the children?

HARRISON

You—had the children.

JACKIE

You didn't want them?

HARRISON

I didn't think I had a choice.

JACKIE

        (*Angry*)
God in heaven!—
        (*Silence. Quietly. Crosses to* HARRISON)
Really—you didn't want them? Would you rather—now
—they didn't exist?

HARRISON

They do exist.

JACKIE

Yes—but if we hadn't . . .

HARRISON

We did.
        (*Silence*)

JACKIE

        (*Softly. Crosses above to right of center
        chair*)
Yes. Something you can be thankful for—you don't have

to get a divorce. Save yourself a lot of money—and save
me the . . . He won't insist you marry him?

> (HARRISON *crosses to fireplace, glass on
> mantel*)

Sorry!

> (SHE *drinks some of her scotch*)

You see—if I once let myself—if I begin to take this—any
of this—seriously—I might begin to scream—

> (*Crosses, sits chest*)

You went to bed with him. You did—make love—to him.
It could be rather funny. Can't you hear them—"Poor
Jackie—did you know? Her husband left her for another
man." Isn't that funny? I think it has a certain quality—
you might say—surprise. Would you say—surprise?

> (*Silence*)

Alan!

> (HARRISON *walks to* JACKIE. SHE *presses
> herself against* HARRISON, *putting her arms
> around his back.* HARRISON *accepts the em-
> brace awkwardly*)

Sit down. Please—will you?

HARRISON

> (*Sits next to* JACKIE)

If you knew I was unfaithful . . .

JACKIE

> (*Quickly*)

I didn't know.

HARRISON

You had a pretty good idea.

JACKIE

> (*Quietly*)

Yes.

HARRISON

Why didn't you throw me out?

JACKIE

I thought it was probably my fault. I never was
much good in bed. It didn't seem—well—altogether
fair I should blame you entirely—and anyway—I never
thought . . .
    (*Silence. Smiling. Leans towards him*)
You've got a kind face, sir. Give a poor girl a kiss.
    (*Silence. Pulls back*)
Actually, you've got rather a silly face. Sweet, of course.
Look—you don't have to sit there—if you don't want to.
God forbid—you should do anything . . .
    (SHE *drinks some of her scotch. Rises,*
    crosses above to below armoir)
I thought this would help. Funny—you want to know
something? It doesn't help a bit. What's on the telly?
    (*Silence. Crosses right of center chair*)
Somehow—I never thought you'd get around—to leav-
ing. I thought you needed me—and what you couldn't
find in bed with me—you were taking care of that.

HARRISON

How could you accept—how could you do that—to yourself?

JACKIE

Yes—I was quite surprised.
    (*Silence. Abruptly*)
It wasn't my immediate reaction.
    (SHE *looks at her empty glass. Turns to-*
    ward kitchen)
Shall I have another?

HARRISON

I don't think so.

JACKIE

(*Turns downstage*)

At first—I thought—I'd kill you—then—I'd kill myself.
All rather melodramatic, I'm afraid. Then—I thought
—go away some place—just disappear—and then—I'd
take the children, bag and baggage, leave you, find a
place to live and make a life for them—and then—do
nothing.

(*Crosses down right center*)

I was wrong! I stood out there tonight more than an
hour—watching this house. I dodged round corners, hid
in the darkness. Sometimes I felt an idiot—sometimes—
I felt ashamed.

(*Silence. Crosses to kitchen, refills glass,
crosses down right center*)

I really would quite like another drink. What kind of
thing is that? Running after your husband—to find out
where he goes! Ask him—if you want to know. That's
what normal people do. People who talk to each other—
trust each other.

HARRISON

I trusted you.

JACKIE

(*Violently*)

Never to make a fuss. Keep a safe distance from the
awkward question. Yes—you trusted me! I stood and
watched you walk into this house. I didn't try to stop
you. I watched the windows—every window was a bedroom and you were making love—and I was—watching.
The pictures in my mind! Always with a girl, of course.

I didn't know then what was really going on—and just as well! I would have thrown up in the gutter—seeing all the pictures he put in my mind. Why did he do that, Alan?

(*Silence. Crosses above center chair, sits upstage arm*)

You think we'll all just go away. Keep quiet long enough and let us talk—we'll all get bored and leave you—and then, the noise will stop? Alan—the noise is in your mind. It isn't us.

(*Silence*)

I know some things about you. More than twenty years?

(*Puts glass down on small table*)

Even I can understand a little of the pain. I can't help take it all away. Once—I thought I could. I was so arrogant when I married you.

(*Abruptly*)

I had the feeling—as I walked into this room—now—you've done this and you can't go back. You can never be the same—quite the same person. This is a thing the woman you thought you were could not have done—and so—you're not that woman. Do you understand what I'm saying?

(JACKIE *rises, crosses and sits next to* HAR-RISON, *takes his hands in hers*)

I can change—Alan—I can be anything you want me to be. If there's hope. There is—isn't there? Hope? Some hope?

HARRISON

I should have left you long ago. I didn't have the strength—and—yes, I was frightened.

(HARRISON *tries to release his hands.*
JACKIE *holds on to him tightly*)

JACKIE

You're not—you can't—leave me? I wasn't asking—will you stay with me? You are—you're going to—stay with me?

HARRISON

Jackie—it doesn't make any sense. I told you—
        (*Desperately. Rises*)
how many times . . .

JACKIE

        (*Violently*)
Once!
        (*Silence. Rises*)
You have to say it once—and clearly. So I hear the words. So I know I didn't—misunderstand—and let you go—when you really meant to stay—just—wanted me to ask.

HARRISON

Why does it have to be so painful?

JACKIE

Pulling people into pieces—isn't that always—painful? God in heaven! What do you want me to do? Send you away with a kiss on the forehead—a pat on the bottom? I have got feelings.
        (JACKIE *lets go of* HARRISON's *hands and turns away from him, laughing. Crosses center*)
I didn't say that! Did you hear what you made me say? Alan—this is ridiculous! What are we doing in this dreadful room? Are you going to live here? You'll go raving mad.

(JACKIE *crosses up center and gestures at
the psychedelic pop art posters*)
Is that the kind of thing he likes?

HARRISON

(*Crosses down left*)
Jackie—for pity's sake!

JACKIE

(*Harshly*)
I don't have any pity. Alan—I hope he takes you—really
breaks you into bits. Why should I pity you?

HARRISON

(*Smiling*)
Do you have to hate me?

JACKIE

(*Crosses right center*)
Does it matter? Do you care?
(*Silence. Slowly*)
I suppose you do. You'll have to see me—coming to col-
lect the children—yes—you wouldn't want to meet me—
hating you. I suppose—if I don't greet you—smiling—
sweetness and light—you won't ever come to see us.
Still—it's not for long. I mean—right now—Michael's
old enough—you can meet him for a drink—a meal.
Betty . . .
(*Silence*)
I'm not sure I want you seeing too much of her. I'll have
to think about it.
(*Quietly*)
If you're going to leave us—live this extraordinary life
—that's your decision. Betty's still a child. I have to think
for her. I'm not sure it's a good idea she should see you

very often—if at all. When people hear about this—well
—they're bound to talk and I think that's enough for the
child to cope with. Her friends at school . . .

(*Silence*)

I shall divorce you, Alan. I don't want to have your name
—not any more. You'll have to support me—and the
children, of course—you'd do that anyway. But I can't
start to work again. It's been too long and I'm feeling
rather old. I think—perhaps—we'll move. I don't want
to go on living in that house. What plans have you
made? Are you going to live here? I presume you'll leave
the firm. You won't want to face . . .

(*Silence. Crosses down center*)

There won't be many of your friends you'll want to see.
Still—I don't suppose you care. Not many of them you
like. Most of them—business friends—and you won't
need them, when you leave the firm. Starting a new life!
You'll find new friends. In a way—I have to admire you
—at your age—making this break. If you'd really thought
about it—then—I might admire you.

HARRISON

I've thought about it.

JACKIE

(*Crosses to* HARRISON)

You can't do this. You can't leave me on my own. I can't
manage, Alan—all on my own. What can I do? Tell me—
please—what do you want me to do? You always said—
making love to me—the world just went away—you said
—and everything was silent. It can be like that—surely—
it can—if you'll help me.

(JACKIE *puts an arm around his neck and
pulls* HARRISON's *face down towards her.*
SHE *kisses him fiercely. Urgently*)

Tell me—what shall I do?
> (*Whispering*)

What would you like me to do? There's isn't anything—Alan—you can ask and I won't do for you. I want to make you happy. Ask me—please—my darling—what shall I do? I only want to make you happy.
> (HARRISON *pulls his face away, turns down-stage.* JACKIE *hits him on upstage shoulder*)

Don't do that! Is it so disgusting? Does it offend you—kissing me? You made love to me three nights ago. Did it make you sick? Did you think of him when you were making love to me—is that how you made yourself—able —to make love? . . .
> (*Silence. Harshly*)

If you can't fuck the one you want to fuck—you can at least think about him . . . You are queer aren't you? I suppose you always were.
> (*Crosses below chest*)

Christ!—what sort of idiot . . . Did you ever make love to me—days when you made love to him?
> (*Silence*)

All the nights you couldn't make love—I blamed myself. I wasn't attractive—clever enough—I didn't know how to make you want me—how to seduce you! The times I went to sleep—knowing I was so inadequate a lover, I couldn't even make my husband hard. No wonder then you couldn't satisfy me. The years we've been married and you never left me really satisfied.

HARRISON

> (*Quietly*)

You came to bed smelling of children. You made love to me like a mother—comforting a child who made unreasonable demands—which had to be endured. One night I wanted to make love. I put my arms around you—

kissed you—and you said—"Darling—before we start—
will you just see—is Betty still asleep? She's been so odd
today, I think she must be coming down with 'flu'." I
was halfway on top of you—and you said . . . The bed
has never lost the smell of children. All your clothes—
your body—the smell sticks to you. It has since they were
born and you said—"I don't want any help. We can't afford it—anyway, I want to do it all myself."

JACKIE

Was that wrong?

HARRISON

We could afford it.

JACKIE

Doing it myself—was that wrong? Why didn't you tell
me?

HARRISON

Why didn't you ask me? Eight years—talking to babies
—when did you talk to me? Jackie—you dressed them—
undressed them—walked with them in the park. You
nursed them and your breasts still smell of milk. You
changed them—held the messes in your hands. Smell
your hands. Can you . . . on your hands—can you smell?
    (*Silence*)
The children are more secure now than I have ever
been. They sleep in the dark. They hide in tiny cup-
boards. They run to strangers. I needed so much more
than them. I needed you—and they had you—and
couldn't let you go. Why should they? Children need
their mother—and their mother . . . The trouble is—of
course—I look human like any other man—a reasonable
and rational—adult, human being—able to cope with all

his problems—buying a house—paying the bills—making the money for you all to spend—giving you presents—asking—
> (*Abruptly*)

love me. When was it ever quiet enough for you to hear? Where was the understanding—help—I needed? Love and tenderness.
> (*Silence*)

I knew it was foolish, weak—unmanly. I couldn't admit everything—each day of my life—frightened me to tears —and I couldn't even cry.
> (*Silence*)

JACKIE

> (*Hesitantly*)

I love you.

HARRISON

I know—yes—of course.

JACKIE

> (*Step toward* HARRISON)

If you could've told me . . . Alan—if you could have said you felt—left out—you felt—I was neglecting you . . .

HARRISON

> (*Quietly*)

I did say—Jackie—I told you—almost every day. You couldn't hear.
> (*Smiling*)

The children make more noise than Clapham Junction. How could you hear?

JACKIE

> (*Vehemently*)

I can't—Alan—please! Don't make me say—I could've

kept you—we'd still be—together—if the children—if I hadn't . . . I love them. They are the best of me.

HARRISON

(*Crosses to* JACKIE)
I don't want you to say that. I don't think it's true. They're very probably—the best of me.

JACKIE

(JACKIE *pushes her hand through* HARRISON*'s arm and links her two hands around it*)
It's almost over. Michael's grown up—with his own life. I hardly ever see him—he's so busy. Betty—she wants to leave school next year and get a job. They'll both of them live away from home. We'll be on our own again.
(*Goes into* HARRISON*'s arms*)
We didn't always have the children. We were happy then. We can—I know we can—Alan—can't we—be happy?

HARRISON

Pretend it's 1953. Pretend—we just got married and we're twenty. Live all kinds of lies—because we can't cope with what we are—what we've made ourselves?
(HARRISON *holds her away. Softly*)
Is that what you want to do?

JACKIE

How do you intend to cope? Hiding yourself in ever-lasting, short and furtive love affairs! How long will this one last? How long have any of them—and you came back—always!—you came back to me.

HARRISON

I never left you.

JACKIE

You haven't left me now.

HARRISON

You—haven't let go.
(*Silence*)

JACKIE

(*Harshly*)
You want to leave me.
(JACKIE *lets go of* HARRISON *and steps back*)
That's all it is. You've decided—and nothing's going to stop you. You won't even let yourself think what you're doing—to me—to the children.
(*Shouting to* HARRISON)
You can't leave me. Don't you understand? Twenty years now! More than half my life! You belong to me.
(*Silence*)

HARRISON

I don't love you.

JACKIE

(*Harshly*)
Alan—you haven't loved me for fifteen years. You stayed with me. What's so different—now—why do you have to love me?

HARRISON

I love him.

JACKIE

(*Backs away*)
Aren't you just a bit too old—talking about love—telling yourself—I am in love—and that makes anything I do—

all right—justified—in the eyes of heaven—sacred! What
am I doing? Begging you to stay!
        (*Crosses center*)
Christ—if you were a man—halfway mature—
        (*Viciously*)
Michael is more grown up than you are—more a man.
        (*Silence*)

HARRISON

Jackie—please. Go home.

JACKIE

You're going to stay here?

HARRISON

        (*Crosses to fireplace*)
Yes.

JACKIE

        (*Crosses to down left chair, picks up
        coat, crosses to center chair, putting coat
        on*)
You'll find love and tenderness with him? With all the
anger—ugliness—he has inside—you expect him to be
gentle—understanding?

HARRISON

        (*Crosses to down left chair*)
I don't want to talk about him.

JACKIE

        (*Smiling*)
No. What shall I tell the children?

HARRISON

I'll come and see them. I think I should tell them myself
—don't you?

JACKIE

What will you tell them?

HARRISON

We're going to live apart.
(*Silence*)

JACKIE

(*Picks up purse*)
We will see each other? You don't intend—we never meet again?

HARRISON

I'll come and see the children. You'll be there?

JACKIE

(*Crosses right of chair, finishes drink.
Quietly*)
Yes.

HARRISON

There's a lot of things we have to talk about.

JACKIE

I suppose there are—yes—what about your clothes? What shall I do with them? Have you brought anything?—did you pack a suitcase?
(*Anger*)
Did you?

HARRISON

No.

JACKIE

Just what you're wearing? Oh, love—not even a clean shirt.

HARRISON

I haven't thought—I didn't—think . . .

JACKIE

(*Crosses above center chair*)
Will we be friends?

HARRISON

I don't know.

JACKIE

(*Crosses up center. Abruptly*)
Why did you wait so long?

HARRISON

I'm sorry.

JACKIE

Before you knew me—you must have known—eventually . . .

HARRISON

(*Smiling*)
How could I know—before I knew you?

JACKIE

When you were a child—didn't you—play—with other boys? Didn't you know? Is it possible—you can be queer and not know? Live so long . . .

HARRISON

(*Quietly*)
I don't know.

JACKIE

Well—you really had me fooled!
(*Silence*)
When will you see the children?

HARRISON

Tomorrow?

JACKIE

(*Opens door*)

Saturday? Yes—all right. I'll see they both stay home. I won't be there. Will you manage?

(HARRISON *nods his head*)

This is even smaller than the flat we used to live in. How will you survive?

(*Silence*)

You'll let me go? You won't even try to stop me? I keep expecting . . .

(JACKIE *turns and walks out of the flat.*
SHE *leaves the door open.*
Silence.
The sound of the front door, as it opens and then closes.
HARRISON *stands for a moment, then walks toward the door.*
HE *stares at the photo-montage on the wall.*
HARRISON *steps forward, kneels on the bed and reaches to tear the faces off the wall.*
HARRISON *murmurs angrily to himself, grunting with the effort, exerting himself violently, tearing his fingernails across the photographs, rasping them down the wall*)

CURTAIN

ACT III

HARRISON sits in center chair, smoking. Silence.
The door opens quietly. HARRISON listens expect-
antly. POWELL looks in.

POWELL

Hello. Are you still here?

HARRISON

Hello.
(*Silence*)

POWELL

(*Closes door*)
Where's Julie? Gone and left you—all on your own?
(*Crosses above center chair*)
You've been having sort of a busy night down here.
(POWELL *looks at the scraps of torn photo-
graphs and smiles*)
Cleaning house?
(HARRISON *crosses to up left chair, puts on
jacket.*
POWELL *glances around at* HARRISON, *takes
picture off wall*)
I always thought it was a bit tactless—keeping all those
photographs—pinning them up where anyone can see
them. When will Julie be back? You do expect him to
come back?

HARRISON

(*Sits up left chair, cigarette from packet,
relights from old cigarette*)
I don't know. Yes, I do.

POWELL

(*Sprawls on bed*)
Are you going to move in with Julie? Good thing if you
did. He shouldn't be left on his own. Some of us—I think
we're probably better—on our own. Julie—gets into all
sorts of trouble.
(*Silence*)
I'm not his brother. Did he tell you?

HARRISON

Yes.

POWELL

Must have been pretty obvious. You're clever enough to
know when you've interrupted—
(*Smiling*)
something. No point trying to kid you. I could've told
him that—the silly bitch!—and I hardly know you.
(*Rolls on tummy*)
You were talking sort of loud. One time—I thought I
heard a woman's voice. Was there a woman here? Is that
what you were fighting about? Do you like to make it
with women as well?
(*Sits up, leans on elbow*)
I make it with women. Not too often—just—when I have
to.
(HARRISON *rises, crosses down left, puts
old cigarette out in ashtray*)
It's not so bad. Sometimes I could almost say I enjoy it.

'Course, if they make a lot of fuss—try and take you over—then you have to show them—make it clear—you know? Are you serious about Julie?

(*Silence*)

You don't have a whole lot to say for yourself.

HARRISON

(*Crosses to fireplace*)

I think perhaps it would be better if you came back to-morrow. Talk to Julie in the morning.

POWELL

I'm coming back tomorrow. I have a date with Julie. He's spending the weekend with me. Don't you remember? You were here.

(*Silence. Smiling*)

Sorry 'bout that! First come—if you'll pardon the expression—first served.

(*Pats bed*)

Come and sit here. Come on. I'd much rather talk to you. I think you're sort of interesting.

(*Silence. Lies back*)

I could've been angry, you know—the way you interrupted—making Julie throw me out—but—I'll forgive you. I'm not jealous. Share and share alike—that's what I say. Don't be greedy. Something I saw once written on a bus—

(*Holds arms up toward ceiling*)

'If you've had some—smile.'

(*Sits up*)

I've had some—and I'm smiling.

(*Silence*)

Do you want to fuck?

(HARRISON *puts cigarette out*)

You think Julie's good—

> (POWELL *swings legs over, sits left of bed*)

I'll show you things that make Julie look an amateur.

> (POWELL *rises, crosses behind* HARRISON,
> *holds him on his upper arms*)

If you're frightened Julie might come back—we can go
up to my room. Darling—don't be shy. I'll tell you what
I like to do . . .

> (HARRISON *turns quickly, lunges at* POW-
> ELL, *and sends him staggering back up-
> stage.*
> *Laughing*)

I like enthusiasm, darling . . .

> (HARRISON *lunges after* POWELL, *reaching
> for his throat.* THEY *fall on to the bed*)

. . . this is ridiculous!

> (*Suddenly,* POWELL *is frightened.* HE *tries
> to pull himself free, clawing at* HARRISON'S
> *hands*)

You're choking me.

> (HARRISON *tightens his grip on* POWELL'S
> *throat.*
> *Incoherent sounds rasp out of his throat.*
> *Gasping*)

Let go. Let—go. Please . . .

> (*Violently, desperately,* POWELL *swings
> his arms up against* HARRISON'S *arms and
> breaks the hold* HARRISON *has on his throat.*
> POWELL *falls on to the floor and rolls away.*
> HE *scrambles up on to his feet, lunging to-
> wards the armoir.* POWELL *faces* HARRISON,
> *who rises, crosses left center*)

What the hell d'you think you're doing? You could've
killed me.

HARRISON

(*Quietly*)

I wanted to kill you.

POWELL

Why? 'Cause I touched you? 'Cause I wanted you to fuck? What is it, darling—saving yourself for Julie?

(HARRISON *starts for* POWELL)

(*Reading*)

Are you going to behave? Couple of things I want to show you.

(*Crosses to armoir, opens door*)

Things might interest you.

(*Crosses to bed, gets folder, dumps stuff out of it*)

Things about Julie. Starting life together—you shouldn't have any secrets. Isn't that what they say? I'll tell you a couple of Julie's secrets. Would you like that? No—I don't think you will. I'm going to tell you anyway. There's so much I don't really know where to start.

(POWELL *takes a notebook*)

I'll give you a taste. You can read the rest of it yourself. I think you'll enjoy it more. I spent a very happy morning—some of it is sort of wild—if you like that kind of thing. A lot of it I don't understand. Some of it simply doesn't make any sense. The bits I like . . .

(POWELL *reads quickly down a page. Reading*)

'A spade—with a handle fourteen inches long.' In all fairness, darling—I should tell you—I haven't read them carefully. It's just pot luck. I don't know them well enough to find the best stuff all the time.

(*Reading*)

Young man seeks interesting part-time occupation. There's a telephone number—650-5372.

(*Looks at phone, then at* HARRISON)

If you don't like the food at home, eat out occasionally. Put yourself in my place, you'll enjoy it. I'll make your body beautiful—no apparatus required—no discrimination.

(*Silence.*

HARRISON *crosses to down left chair*)

Goes on for half a page!

(POWELL *reads quickly down the page.*

Crosses below chest)

The man was awkward, hesitant. I opened the door. He almost turned away. It was ridiculous . . . I thought—at least—knowing he's come to fuck—all he has to do is pay—

(HARRISON *sits down left chair*)

at least he'll be decisive.

(*Reading. Crosses down left center*)

Loving in the night of dying.

(*Turns the page, reading*)

Naturally—he assumed—I had all the experience. I would take control—seduce him. Offering all manner of mysterious delights. Five pounds down—and rapture guaranteed. I pulled the curtains—asked—what shall I do? What do you like? I thought—he's bound to notice —I don't even know the words. He wanted me to take off all my clothes . . . He wanted just to look at me, he said. At first—he wanted just to look. He began to get excited—and then—he took control. It was as I imagined it would be. No feeling—it wasn't my body—no guilt—I belonged to him—no self—I didn't exist.

(*Silence. Turns pages, looking*)

I thought he'd give us some more detail.

(*Turns the page. Reading. Turns downstage*)

When the punishment is shame and there is no shame—
how can the punishment begin? How can it ever end?

(POWELL *turns the pages quickly. Crosses
to up left chair, brings it close to* HARRI-
SON, *sits. Reading*)

November 18th. The telephone woke me. A fat man.
Almost impotent. Made me sick. My face so close to
the flaccid, dead heaviness, of his thighs. The belly
mound. Once. He wanted to stay. 3:30 P.M. A young
man. Tall and dark. Big. Frightening. Twice. 5 P.M. A
businessman, I think. Lonely. Excited. Middle-aged. He
wanted me to fuck him. The silly bitch. Once. Pages of
this.

(*Reading*)

Pretty one. Waiting on the road. We talked. Went home
with him. Strange—and sad—he cried a lot. Oh, mother
—he was so my own, own brother.

(*Throws book to* HARRISON)

What the hell is that!

(*Rises, crosses to bed, searches for another book, finds it*)

I wish I could find the one I was reading this morning.
It's sort of interesting, isn't it? Somehow—you wouldn't
expect Julie—doesn't seem tough enough.

(*Silence*)

Are you listening, darling? I wouldn't want you to miss
anything.

(*Smiling. Crosses to small chair*)

I could have you now. You wouldn't even try to stop
me.

(*Puts chair back upstage*)

Funny—'cause now—I don't really want you.

(HARRISON *holds the notebook in his*
hands, his arms hanging loosely in front
of him.

POWELL *crosses and sits center chair, one*
foot on foot stool. Reading)

December 27th. I haven't spoken to anyone now for
three days. I've been sitting here in my room. I read for
a while. Most of the time—nothing. It has been very
quiet. At five o'clock today the telephone rang. I didn't
answer. Doesn't that make you want to cry? The silly
bitch! I was here that whole bloody Christmas.

(*Looks at* HARRISON. *Then—reading*)

Gordon was filthy to me all night. Kept laughing at me.
Told stories about me to his friends. Told them all the
things he made me do. After we finished dinner—he
showed some pornographic films. He sent me to the
bedroom with a friend of his—an old man—told me—'I
want him to enjoy himself. Julie—he's a very dear old
friend of mine.' He could hardly make it. I was there almost an hour—and then, he said—'Yes—it was all right.
Nothing to make a lot of fuss about, dear boy.' Gordon
said—'Julie—you should have tried a little harder. Now
—I shall have to punish you'—and he hit me with a
cane. He made me take off all my clothes and he hit me
with a cane. He hit me . . .

(*Half-smiling*)

Sort of party you read about—and never get invited to.
Darling, that isn't all. That isn't half. Wait 'til I find . . .

(POWELL *turns the page and reads quickly*
down it. Reading)

After the other men went home, Gordon kissed me—
said—would I be gentle with him—take off his clothes—
wash him and oil him—powder—put him to bed. 'All the
excitement, Julie—now—I feel so tired. We won't make

love tonight.' He reached to pat my face and said—'You were such a good boy tonight. Behaved yourself quite beautifully'—and I pushed my thumbs into his eyes. I forced my nails through the soft, staring wetness—into his head. His blood—the obscene jelly of his brains—spilled on my hands. I threw him off the bed. I put my foot down on his stomach—walked on his chest. I felt the bones break—splintering—underneath my feet. I pushed my heel hard into his mouth. I felt his teeth drive deep into my flesh. I knelt beside him—whispered what I would do before I would let him die. I cut across his stomach—opened his body—thrust the knife inside.

> (*Silence.* POWELL *puts book down on foot stool, rises, walks to counter, gets a drink. Silence.* POWELL *crosses to table, sits.*
> *The door opens and* WESTON *walks into the flat.* HE *stops abruptly*)

WESTON

> (*Up center*)

Dear God in heaven! What's been going on? What have you been doing?

> (HARRISON *looks at* WESTON, *holding the notebook against his chest.*
> WESTON *looks at the notebooks on the bed, the photographs torn from the wall and the general confusion in the room*)

POWELL

Hello, Julie.

> (WESTON *turns and looks across the room at* POWELL, *who is holding a glass of scotch*)

I was wondering when would you get back.

> (*Silence.* WESTON *looks at* HARRISON)

WESTON
(*Shuts door*)
If you want to read it, love—don't let me stop you.

POWELL
We've already looked at quite a lot of them.

WESTON
(*Crosses center*)
Alan?
(HARRISON *half-turns away from* WESTON
and opens the notebook)

POWELL
We've been entertaining ourselves—waiting for you—

WESTON
(*To* POWELL)
Was that your idea?

POWELL
Of course it was. He didn't know anything about them.
I thought—starting out together—you shouldn't have secrets from each other. Gives you such an unfair ad-
vantage. Don't you think?

WESTON
Was it a lot of fun?

POWELL
Full of surprises.

WESTON
I can imagine.

POWELL
Lot of things I missed the first time through.

WESTON

(*Crosses by bed*)

Did you—was that . . .

> (WESTON *gestures at the ruined photo-
> montage and the scattered scraps of pho-
> tographs*)

. . . your idea too?

POWELL

That was your friend's idea. I got here in time to stop
him pulling the whole place to pieces. You should be
thankful.

WESTON

(*Harshly*)

Davy—go home—will you? Get the hell out of here!

POWELL

Miss all the fun?

WESTON

Darling—the fun starts when I get hold of you and cut
your balls off—I mean—cut them off! I can imagine things
to do with you that'd make anything you read sound
like a fairy tale.

> (HARRISON *begins to read aloud from the
> notebook*)

HARRISON

(*Reading*)

'. . . stranger here. We haven't seen you before.' He
was a small man and he wore a faded, almost yellow
overall. He smiled. I think he was embarrassed. I think
he plays his game of jokes and camaraderie, because he
cannot make another way to deal with the endless story

of disease, decay and degradation. He wrote my name and told me to sit down. He smiled at me. There was contempt inside the smile—disgust—if I wanted to look —and if I didn't—it was there anyway.

WESTON

>   (*Turns to* HARRISON)

Read it all, love.

>   (WESTON *crosses to* HARRISON *and takes
>   the notebook.* WESTON *turns the page, looks
>   at the words written on the page. Crosses
>   to chest, sits*)
>   (*Reading*)

'Yes—it sounds like gonorrhea. Let's have a look.'

>   (POWELL *crosses right center*)

He was a very young man, detached, professional, not at all involved. I unzipped my trousers, showed myself to him. What did he see? 'I think we'll have a test. There's not a lot of doubt.' He turned away and wrote on bits of paper. 'Wash your hands.' He gestured with his head. He didn't look at me. The water in the tap ran very hot—scalding my hands. I held them in the water.

>   (*Silence. Turns page*)

Talking—to ask—asking—to know . . . knowing—to understand and hoping—hoping—hoping. Looking—to see . . . listening—to hear . . . touching—to feel and holding—holding—holding. Searching—to find . . . finding—to have . . . having—to keep and loving—loving —loving.

>   (*Glances at* HARRISON)

He looked through a microscope—he looked at me— smeared across a narrow piece of glass. He looked inside me. What did he see? He made me bend across a high,

hard couch and punched a hypodermic needle into my
buttock—into my body—into my rotting soul—and shame
—I was ashamed.

POWELL

Yes.

WESTON

(*Smiling*)
Does that make you sick? Darling—that doesn't begin
to tell you what it was like! I've done things that would
really turn your stomach. I've been to bed with you.
I've touched you. I've let you touch me. Think about
that. If anything is going to make you sick!
(*Rises, turns to* POWELL)
Have you any idea, darling—just how bad you smell?
Has no one ever told you? Standing in the same room
makes me want to take a bath in disinfectant. Your
clothes stink. Don't you ever wash? Do you have any
idea how ugly you are? Kissing you is like swimming
underwater in a sewer. Anyone goes to bed with you—
he's got to be pretty desperate.

POWELL

You went to bed with me.

WESTON

Darling—last night—I would have fucked a pig.
(*Starts to laugh*)

POWELL

You vicious, degenerate—evil . . .

WESTON

(*Calmly*)
You cock-sucking, mother-fucking cunt.

(*Silence*)

Does that give you some idea, darling—how I feel about you? What sort of chance you have—hanging about— hoping to get into me?

POWELL

I don't want to—get into you! You're diseased. You're— depraved . . .

WESTON

Right. All those good things.

POWELL

If I'd known . . . if I'd had any idea . . .

WESTON

You're in no danger, darling. The good doctors cured me—and I've been a lot more careful since. Until last night, of course. Nothing I've done this year I regret so much as letting you in here last night—letting you— fuck me.

POWELL

You won't get another chance.
> (POWELL *walks out of the flat.*
> WESTON *shuts the door, puts hat on hook.*
> *Silence*)

WESTON

Oh, love.
> (*Silence.*
> HARRISON *rises, crosses to foot stool takes book and tears it. Crosses to bed, tears up books and papers. Takes folder and book, crosses to table tearing folder and book.*
> WESTON *walks forward center*)

HARRISON

(*Harshly, leaning on table*)
Stay there, Julie. Stay where you are. Stay away.

WESTON

I don't know what else I'm going to say. Some of the
things I wrote—if it helps you—
(*Abruptly*)
—the worst things—anger at you—and hatred, all of
that—they didn't happen.

HARRISON

Ugliness.

WESTON

I can't start defending all the things I've done.
(*Angrily*)
I don't have to. It's none of your bloody business. You
weren't here.

HARRISON

I don't know—with all the words—Julie—all the pictures . . .

WESTON

(*Crosses to below chest*)
Nobody says you have to stay. I don't want you—staying
—if it means you punish me for everything I've done. I
want to send you away. If I didn't love you—Christ!—I
know I should. You have to understand—reading those
things sickens—and disgusts you—reading! They happened to me. It's possible I manage pretty well—punish-
ing myself. Do you want to go?

HARRISON

(*Turning*)

I want this—not to have happened.

WESTON

Coming here tonight?

HARRISON

Finding you—with him—fighting with you—and Jackie
—all the bitterness—reading . . .
  (*Silence. Sit table*)
It has happened.

WESTON

You made it happen.

HARRISON

I did all kinds of things tonight—leaving the house. I
told myself—I'm doing this for the last time—walking
down the stairs—listening to the sounds around the
house—the gramophone playing in Betty's room—doors
opening and closing—kitchen noises—cars on the street
outside. I've lived in that house for eleven years. I've
made a lot of changes—made it my house—you wouldn't
recognize the house I bought—and now—pulling open
the front door—for the last time—I thought.

WESTON

  (*Crosses, sits in chair, center*)
Coming here tonight—was that supposed to be some
sort of ending?

HARRISON

Leaving it all behind—yes—walking away . . .

WESTON

How could it be? In your head—maybe. Did you think
she'd just—let you go? Wish you good luck and wave!
You didn't even tell her you were leaving.

HARRISON

(*Angrily*)

I couldn't tell her. Until I saw you—I didn't know myself.

WESTON

You didn't leave home just to live with me? You didn't?
I mean—if you did—hadn't you better think about it?
How long do you think this is going to last? I won't be
a comfort to you in your old age.
(*Rises, crosses away left*)
There's nothing I hate more than old, painted queens—
(*Picks up papers*)
—and you're a whole lot older, love—than I am. Twenty
years? You haven't worn particularly well. You haven't
taken care of yourself. You've lost your hair. You're getting soft. And smoking the way you do! How long will
your heart put up with that? What d'you think—I'm going to spend my life nursing an old man? Anyway, you'll
soon get bored with me. I'm sort of stupid, when you
get to know me. I'm not really meant to live with people,
I've decided. Something happens in my head—I expect
. . . all sorts of idiotic things. It takes a lot of strength—
living with me—and you're not very strong. I'm not sure
you've got the strength to make it—being queer. You
meet a lot of funny people.
(*Crosses above center chair*)
You don't intend we sit here the rest of our lives—the
two of us—together!
(*Puts papers into trash can*)
Doesn't that sound sort of draggy?
(*Crosses to armoir, takes off sweater, hangs
it up, shuts door*)
Another thing—you could easily go back to girls. You've

had a lot of practise. Since you can make it either way—
it's easier with girls—easier to live—you know? People
don't look at you so funny—with your arm around a girl
—even a fella—old as you.

(*Silence. Crosses right center*)

You might go back to her. It's not impossible. You told
each other some home truths tonight. Is that so bad?
Could be the making of a great relationship. A little
while—you might fall in love. I'm an incurable romantic.

(*Harshly, crosses to fireplace*)

Why don't you get out of here? If you're going to sit
there—looking at me—Christ!—I can do without that.
Accusing! What right have you—accusing me?

(*Crosses down left center*)

You think—what?—I failed you? All that stuff—and you
can only see—I failed you? You set some bloody sort of
standard and I'm supposed to live—you're not here to
help me—love me—keep them all away—still—I'm supposed . . . Because you condescend to love me—not to
live with me—at a safe distance—love me—in your head
—where no one else can see—not even me! Listen—you
failed me tonight. You let her scream at me. You didn't
stop her. You didn't try. I made you feel ashamed! I'm
supposed to let her walk in here—say what she likes—
scream at us? She called our making love—filthy! You
wouldn't stand up for yourself—leave alone take care of
me. I thought you were some special sort of thing. I
thought you had decided to leave her, because your life
with her was nothing. I thought—you came here, because you loved me. I didn't understand—you had this
picture in your head—some romantic dream of life with
me—and tenderness—beauty! You can't come here—running away from her—using me. I won't survive, love

—when you run away from me. I've cut off from you—for this moment—free—I can let you go. I want you to go.

(*Silence. Crosses, sit in down left chair*)

It would be easier. I could rest then—be the person I am —not have to try and be this person you have in your crazy head—this—innocent.

HARRISON

When you first went to bed with me, you knew so much about making love—you couldn't have been innocent. I never thought you were.

WESTON

We wouldn't have gone to bed together if I had been innocent.

HARRISON

I meant—without deceit. You tell the truth. I haven't told the truth to anyone in twenty years. I lived deceit and lies, as naturally as smiling. I wanted to escape. I thought perhaps I could.

(*Smiling*)

I'm not sure, if I'd known this whole night had to happen—I'm such a coward—I would most likely have stayed where I was.

(*Bitterly, crosses above chair*)

A strong man wouldn't have done all this. Only someone selfish—knowing what he wanted—disregarding other people's pain—his own responsibility—not looking any way but straight ahead—knowing if he looks around— he has to stop.

(*Silence*)

I used you, Julie. Leaving—I had to go somewhere—go —to someone. I wasn't ready—to go nowhere—on my own.

WESTON

I'm glad you came here.

HARRISON

I shan't go back. There's nothing there.

WESTON

I'm sorry I said those things. I didn't mean them. I was so terrified—knowing you'd read that stuff.

HARRISON

I could have stopped that happening to you. I can only think—

WESTON

(*Hesitantly*)

It didn't happen to me, love—not all of it. I went out and made it happen.

HARRISON

I shall have trouble sometimes, when I think about it—
(*Silence, crosses, sits on foot stool*)
I may want to hurt you.

WESTON

I know that. Christ! Whatever happens—one thing—right? You don't go away. It's worth it, love—I mean—
(*Laughing*)
—speaking for myself, you understand—
(*Doubtful*)
Isn't it worth it? That's what this is all about—yes? Staying together—being together—and no lies.
(*Abruptly*)
Some lies—aren't there always—and—some pain—but not so much—and maybe—less and less—Love—I don't want to hurt you. I'm not angry anymore. I just have to know—

right? Staying—you really are—and loving—whatever happens. We'll tidy all this mess tomorrow—yes?

HARRISON

Tomorrow—I have to see the children.
(*Silence*)
I can't think of Betty crying. I tell myself—she doesn't really care. She'll hardly notice I'm not there. I can't think—tomorrow—when I tell her—she might cry.

WESTON

Oh, love—my love.
(*Silence*)

CURTAIN